Henri Nouwen

Henri Nouwen

A Restless Seeking for God

JURJEN BEUMER

Translated from the Dutch
by David E. Schlaver
and Nancy Forest-Flier

A Crossroad Book
The Crossroad Publishing Company
New York

This printing: 1999

Originally published in Dutch as *Onrustig zoeken naar God: De spiritualiteit van Henri Nouwen* © by Uitgeverij Lannoo, Tielt, Belgium, 1996.

The Crossroad Publishing Company
370 Lexington Avenue, New York, NY 10017

English translation copyright © 1997 by Crossroad Publishing Company

Printed in the United States of America

Library of Congress Cataloging-in-Publication Data
Beumer, Jurjen, 1947-
   [Onrustig zoeken naar God. English]
   Henri Nouwen : a restless seeking for God / Jurjen Beumer ;
translated from the Dutch by David E. Schlaver and Nancy Forest-Flier.
    p. cm.
   ISBN 0-8245-1677-X (hard); 0-8245-1768-7 (pbk.)
   1. Nouwen, Henri J. M. 2. Catholic Church – Clergy – Biography.
3. Nouwen, Henri J. M. – Contributions in spirituality.
4. Spirituality – Catholic Church – History – 20th century.
5. Catholic Church – Doctrines – History – 20th century.   I. Title.
BX4705.N87B4813   1997
282'.092–dc21
  [B]   97-6808

CONTENTS

Part 3
SPIRITUALITY AND ETHICS

Part 4
THEOLOGICAL INSIGHTS

Part 5
AND TAKE YOU WHERE
YOU DO NOT WISH TO GO...

PREFACE

To take a deep interest in someone's life may seem indiscreet at times. The biographer has an eager desire to know more and more, as gradually he does. He is like a voyeur who silently stalks the person and his environment, seeking more data and more facts. This detective work has something insatiable about it, because facts are never enough. There is always some missing detail. Nevertheless, at a certain moment he must stop, because he may not violate the secret of the person he is writing about. A good biography revolves around that very secret. It is that inner secret which links the biography with its readers. The biographer is only an intermediary between the two.

How can I write a book about someone whom I have known very closely for many years, who is a friend of mine? Is it even possible to take the necessary distance? Originally I thought I could construct a meaningful portrait of Henri Nouwen from his books alone. After all, you don't have to know someone personally in order to be able to write about him. On the other hand, it can also be an advantage if you do know him. Throughout our friendship over fifteen years I have walked step by step with Henri Nouwen and his books. I know the themes, and I think I know the passion of his heart.

Perhaps, I continued thinking, this personal relationship actually adds a certain something. I would have direct access to the written sources and to the "object" himself. And I could easily broaden my "research" to people from his own surroundings and meet with them to get to know Henri Nouwen even better. Even so, I kept thinking about the problem of that desired "distance." My potential readers are not waiting for hagiography, for a pious life of a saint. On the contrary, in the midst of a certain

Nouwen-boom and for all the Nouwen adherents in the United States, the time has come for a critical evaluation. In the long run myth-making is crippling for any author.

So I made a kind of compromise with myself. On the one hand I would write about Henri Nouwen as if I had never met him. There is, after all, a mountain of written material with many biographical details which lends itself very well to objective research. This would give me space and the necessary critical distance. On the other hand, I did not want to completely discard my personal connection with Henri. After all, he greatly influenced and enriched my way of doing theology and my faith. His thinking and style of writing have pointed me in new directions, in spite of the fact that I have gone my own way and on certain points have differed with him.

Thus, with a combination of a scholarly approach and my more personal involvement, a picture finally emerges, my picture. It is the same with an artist who paints a portrait. Every artist approaches the task differently. The accents and the personal style play a major role, but so do the inevitable biases and the spirit of the age in which the painter lives. And then there are the signals transmitted from subject to artist. There is a subtle influencing between the two of them that shapes and defines the artistic quality of the work.

I begin my "portrait" of Henri Nouwen with the hope that many who come to admire it will want to go in the direction pointed to by its subject: that is, to the Source from which our life springs and wells up.

This book was finished but was not yet at the printer when Henri Nouwen died, suddenly and completely unexpectedly, on Saturday, September 21, 1996, in the land of his birth, the Netherlands. On September 24 we bade him farewell at a Eucharist at the cathedral church of St. Catharine in Utrecht. On Saturday, September 28, 1996, he was buried in Toronto.

My publisher and I decided not to change the text of the book. It was not necessary. All of Nouwen's life's journey is covered in this biography and all of his life's work is treated, except for those things which were still to come, the subjects I know he would have liked to have written about but no longer could. In any event, no human life, no volume of work, is ever completed. I did add my own *In Memoriam* at the very end of the book, a personal impression of Henri Nouwen's last days.

I want very much to thank a number of people for their assistance and support. First Henri Nouwen's father, Mr. L. J. M. Nouwen of Geysteren, the Netherlands. He supplied for me the biographical details which could not be found in Nouwen's books. He also allowed me to freely examine the family albums, and most of the photos in this book come from those albums. I would like to thank Louis ter Steeg and Maria ter Steeg-Van Wayenburg, who read this manuscript in an early draft and provided valuable observations. The English translation was the work of Fr. David Schlaver and Nancy Forest-Flier, to whom I am deeply grateful. The help provided by Laurent Nouwen, Henri's youngest brother, made it possible for me to better relate the final events concerning Henri's death.

Finally, I offer my thanks to Henri Nouwen himself. He was not involved with the shape of this book, nor with the text or the contents. But he supported me in writing this biography in every possible way. I will miss him very much. May his memory be a blessing for us.

N.B. The numbers after the citations from Nouwen's works in the text refer to the numbered bibliography at the end of the book. An example: 5:60 — *The Wounded Healer*, page 60. Other references appear in the notes at the end of the book.

JURJEN BEUMER

Haarlem, October 1996

Part 1

THE LIFE OF
HENRI NOUWEN

- 1 -

THE EARLY YEARS

Henri Jozef Machiel Nouwen was born on January 24, 1932, in Nijkerk, a city on the edge of the Veluwe hills in the middle of the Netherlands. He was the first child of Laurent Jean Marie Nouwen, born January 3, 1903, and Maria Huberta Helena Ramselaar, born September 3, 1906. The roots of the Nouwen family were not in Nijkerk but in the south of the Netherlands, in the picturesque, so-called "white city" of Thorn, in the province of Limburg.

The genealogy of the Nouwen family goes back some three hundred years. The Nouwens of old were blacksmiths. They specialized in artistic forge work (locks and ornaments) as well as in the day-to-day work of horseshoeing.

Henri's father came from a family of eleven. Since Laurent's father was the town clerk of Venlo around 1900, his mother had her hands full with the children. Laurent Nouwen, from whom I got a great deal of information about the early family history, described his parents (Henri's grandfather and grandmother) as studious, intelligent, and virtuous. They were incorruptible, pious, and very Catholic. Their authority ran parallel with a somewhat docile mode of behavior, not unusual in those days. That one or more of the children from such a large family would "give their lives" to the faith and the church happened rather regularly.

Henri's mother, Maria Huberta Helena Ramselaar, came from a family of eight children. The Ramselaar family were from Amersfoort, a large city in the middle of the Netherlands. They were gentle people with an artistic bent. The father of Henri's

13

mother died at a young age, but her mother, Henri's grandmother, was an important figure in the family history. This woman's maiden name was Sarah de Munk. Her family came from Alkmaar, and she was spoken about in the family with great respect. She was a very energetic and enterprising woman with great perseverance. She built her late husband's little shop in Amersfoort into a large business which brought the family prosperity. On the religious side the family was also traditional Catholic, but without the pious traits of the Nouwens. The oldest son of the Ramselaar family, Toon, became a priest of the archdiocese of Utrecht. This uncle of Henri would later play an important role in his development.

The Nouwen Family

"There is always that strange tendency in marriage to divide roles, even psychological roles. And our culture certainly encourages that: mother for the children, you for earning a living; mother to be gentle and forgiving, you to be strict and demanding; mother hospitable and receptive, you reserved and selective. In fact, you even liked to play with these differences and point them out in your comments at dinner."
(17:25)

Maria Ramselaar and Laurent Nouwen married in 1931. Their first child, Henri Jozef Machiel, was born nine months later. It was a very difficult delivery, costing the mother and child three days and nights of struggle. Many prayers were offered up on behalf of little Henri. You could say it was a miracle that it all turned out so well, because during the long and strenuous delivery there were moments of fear for the lives of both mother and child. Later a very strong bond grew between mother and son, and considering the difficult beginning this is not at all surprising. Shortly thereafter, in 1934, there followed a second son. After a period of ten years another son and a daughter were born.

A beaming eight-year-old.

Henri (right) at twelve, with his brother Paul.

Henri's Father

*"Father, you are a man with a strong personality, a power-
ful will, and a convincing sense of self. You are known as a
hard worker, a persistent fighter for your clients, and a man
who never loses an argument, or at least will never confess
to losing one! You have achieved what you strove for. Your
successful career has rewarded your efforts richly and has
strengthened you in your conviction that success in life is the
result of hard work. If anything is clear about your life-style,
it is that you want to keep your hands on the tiller of your
ship." (17:45–46)*

Laurent Nouwen, Henri's father, was to become well known in
the juridical world for his expert knowledge of tax law. With
the title of "notarial candidate" he worked for sixteen years as
"inspector of registration and public property."[1] By virtue of this
function, the family lived first in Nijkerk, where Henri was born
in 1932, and later in Venlo and Bussum. After Laurent Nouwen's appointment as a lawyer in The Hague, the family moved
to Scheveningen during the Second World War. In 1959 he was
named professor in notarial and fiscal law at the Roman Catholic University of Nijmegen. He went there to live in 1960. In
1973, when he reached retirement age, he moved back to the
North Limburg town of Geysteren, although he kept working up
to 1982 at the Roermond court.

Henri's Mother

*"Always there was a smile and a tear, joy and sadness. From
the moment of my birth when her tears merged with smiles,
it has always been that way." (12:16).*

After finishing elementary school, Maria Nouwen-Ramselaar,
Henri's mother, earned her secondary diploma in English at a
young age by studying on her own. Next she took up Italian,

which she came to speak fluently, and she enlisted a classics scholar to teach her Latin and Greek in Hoogland, hoping to pass her government examination for the gymnasium (secondary school). But when she got married and went to live in Nijkerk, she was not able to continue her studies. For many years she also worked as head bookkeeper for the family business in Amersfoort, first for her mother and later for her brother. She was a very intelligent and deeply religious woman with a great interest in literature and mysticism. She and her husband made many long journeys together, to Saudi Arabia, Brazil, Mexico, and many other lands. She died in 1978.

Youthful years

"I have always had a strange desire to be different than other people." (9:48)

Henri grew up under the protection of a harmonious and traditional Catholic family. Socially it was the time for rebuilding the Netherlands and all of Western Europe. The enormous damage wrought by the Second World War had to be repaired. The 1950s were industrious years, but they were also very traditional. Norms and values, traditions and customs, all reverted to their proper places, both in the church and in society. In contrast to what many had hoped for during the war years, the political and religious establishment tried to return to conditions as they had existed before the war. The confessional pillars (Roman Catholicism and Protestant Christianity) were rebuilt as if there had been no war. Everyone fell back into the same familiar camp. In 1954, the Catholic church provincial issued a "mandate" to the world as if no other churches existed. The Protestant churches emphasized their singularity as if no ecumenical movement had ever started. Reaction against this lethargic parochialism could not be avoided, with the high point coming in the turbulent year 1968. It was in this context that Henri grew up, first as a child in school, later as a student.

Playing priest as well as Indian.

Along with the societal and religious context naturally comes development of the individual, his particular character, will power, and energy. Henri stands out in this story as an enormously lively child. He was very active, ever in motion, and always busy. From his youngest years he wanted to become a priest. The attic of his family home is still filled with the liturgical toys that he used to "play priest," enlisting other family members as parishioners. A certain piety and devotion seem to have been present in him at a very early age, nourished as they were by his mother and grandmother.

From the beginning of his childhood we can see two sides of his character developing. On the one side was the very energetic and enterprising person; on the other was the person inclined to piety and reflection with a great interest in church life.

Also striking was his passion to provide leadership. He absolutely had to be the leader in everything. Whether it was in playing priest or in other activities, Henri was always the ringleader. His father and mother must have played a role in this ambition to take charge besides having a certain inclination in this direction themselves. They brought up their children with a strong emphasis on independence and critical thinking. In addition, the family was well-off, and because of their father's position the children became accustomed to mixing with well-educated people who were also leaders. All of this made it possible for Henri to develop himself to his full potential — spiritually, socially, and materially. He was definitely not the type to let chances pass him by. A healthy ambition helps to form character and gives a human life clear direction.

Father and Son

"Recently, on looking into a mirror, I was struck by how much I look like my dad." (29:116)

Ambition can also have its negative side in the sense that it drives other people away. Often our strongest side is at the same time our weakest side. Our weak side is usually subtly repressed, and it sometimes comes to the surface very unexpectedly for those most intimate with us. According to his father, this was also true of his son. He was proud of Henri, of his desire for leadership, his ambition, his creative flow of plans and ideas. But he does not deny that all this had its shadow side. There were the sudden flareups, the angry outbursts when someone offended him, when someone dared to challenge his leadership. It is quite fascinating to hear the father talk about his son this way. The father-son relationship is by definition a sensitive one, with its unexpressed competition and its silent battle for precedence. But it is also the hidden dance for the mother's attention, the unconscious attempts to gain her favor.[2]

Mother and Son

> *"I do not think I am exaggerating when I say that it was mother's deep and lasting devotion to the Eucharist that was one of the factors, if not the main factor, in my decision to become a priest."* (17:64)

> *"Years after my mother's death, she continues to bear fruit in my life. I am deeply aware that many of my major decisions since her death have been guided by the Spirit of Jesus, which she continues to send me."* (31:39).

Henri's mother was very much attached to her oldest son. Fighting for both his life and her own at the time of his birth was rewarded with a very intimate relationship.

He let her read everything he wrote and telephoned her frequently. He discussed all his new plans with her. Their correspondence fills many pages and could reveal a great deal about each of them. The mother's affection toward her son grew over the years and deepened gradually as they shared each other's spirituality. When Henri visited his parents in the Netherlands, he celebrated Mass each day with them. Having a son who was a

Henri as a seven-year-old, with his mother and brother Paul.

On a bicycle with his father.

His ordination, 1957.
Henri is second from left.

priest was very important to his mother. His father took more distance, a distance that grew as the mother came closer to the son. The rather sudden death of his mother in 1978 left a deep mark on Henri. These impressions and the parent-child relationships are reflected in Henri's books. As an educated psychologist, he knew what he was talking about. But factual understanding is one thing; experiencing it personally and living through it is something else again. It is here (and we will see this again and again further on) that the strength of his writing is revealed: this ability to combine knowledge with personal experience.

Universal Parenthood

"One of the most beautiful things that can happen in a human life is that parents become brothers and sisters for their children, that children become fathers and mothers for their parents, that brothers and sisters become friends and that fatherhood, motherhood, brotherhood, and sisterhood are deeply shared by all the members of the family at different times and on different occasions." (33:116).

In the book about his mother, *In Memoriam* (12), he bade his mother farewell. Later, many years after her death, he worked out his problems with his father, his actual father as well as the image of that father that had taken up residence within him, his inner father. *The Return of the Prodigal Son* (29) describes this process, a journey which every person must take.

– 2 –

YEARS OF STUDY

Training for the Priesthood and Study of Psychology

When he was eighteen, Nouwen passed his final gymnasium (secondary school) examination at Aloysius College in The Hague. In order to get off to a good start in his studies for the priesthood at the major seminary, he was advised first to enter the final year at the minor seminary in Apeldoorn. One of his mother's brothers was president there. This Uncle Toon, Monsignor A. C. Ramselaar, would later become well known in the Netherlands because of his commitment to Jewish-Christian dialogue, a bitter necessity considering the role of the churches during the Holocaust. He was "the first and for a long time the only person in our country to call the attention of his co-religionists to Israel and Judaism."[3]

After the minor seminary, future priests went to the major seminary. At that time each diocese still had its own program for educating priests. Henri would spend six years as a seminary student at Rijsenburg (near Driebergen), the program for the archdiocese of Utrecht. Two years of philosophy and four years of theology: that was how the priests of that time were educated. In 1957 Nouwen was ordained a priest.

At the end of this seminary program he was assigned by the archbishop of Utrecht, Bernard Alfrink, to gain further expertise in theology at the Gregorian University in Rome. But Nouwen had other plans and presented another program to his bishop, something that would have great consequences for the rest of his life. He offered an alternate suggestion: studying psychology in Nijmegen. Archbishop Alfrink, who later as cardinal would play

a major role in the renewal of the church in the Netherlands, was
not the kind of man to refuse this sort of request from his priests.
In the years that followed (1957–64) Nouwen showed tremendous energy. He immersed himself completely in psychology, not
so much for its scientific value, but because he felt intuitively
that the discipline of psychology dealt with issues that were of
utmost importance for the church and for theology (especially
pastoral theology), issues that had been pushed too far into the
background. The purely human side of faith had become much
too entangled in church structures and ritual, threatening, from a
pastoral point of view, to stifle human development. The famous
psychologist of religion Han Fortmann (1912–70) had a great influence on Nouwen during his studies in Nijmegen. Fortmann was
professor in general and comparative psychology of religion and
culture. His major work, *Als ziende de Onzienlijke* (On seeing
the Invisible, 1964), was pioneering for the time. And that was
no less true for his *Oosterse Renaissance, Kritische reflecties op
de cultuur van nu* (Eastern Renaissance: Critical reflections on the
present culture, 1970).[4] Especially noteworthy in this small book,
often reprinted, is the relationship between action and contemplation in our socially active age. These are themes that we will meet
later in Nouwen's own work.

In the midst of his studies and the joy he felt over these new
insights, Henri also moved beyond the accepted norms. He joined
a work placement program in the mines of South Limburg and
another at Unilever in Rotterdam and served as a chaplain in the
army.[5] He wanted to know and experience what faith meant in
the harsh reality of everyday life. During these years he also discovered traveling, and he would be on the go for the rest of his
life, always moving from here to there, always on the way to yet
another city, to yet another country. At that time he had no means
to finance his travel. He arranged for an unpaid position with
the Catholic Emigration Service as a chaplain for the shipowners
of the Holland-America Line.[6] It was an ideal job for a working student, to serve as a young pastor accompanying people on
the long journey to New York. For travelers at that time these
voyages were not pleasure trips, nor were they plush cruises, for

He spent his whole life in transit and took many trips.
Henri (right) in Jerusalem.

Henri in uniform as a reserve army chaplain in the psychiatric
service in The Hague during his internship in clinical psychology,
1962.

Discovering a new world as chaplain for the Holland-America Line in New York, 1962.

As many remember him, talking with his hands.
The Menninger Foundation, Topeka, Kansas, 1965.

frequently these emigrants settled in the United States or Canada. Pastoral support in this cultural transition was not a luxury.

The United States was an important destination for Nouwen because during his study he had come to know the work of the famous psychologist Gordon Allport. He very much wanted to meet this man personally, and now he had the chance. A letter to Cardinal Cushing of Boston provided him with an introduction to Gordon Allport, who taught at Harvard. Allport was a psychologist who also had an interest in religion and pastoral psychology, contrary to the psychological trends of the time. That coincided with Nouwen's similar longtime interests. The contact took place, and Allport advised Nouwen to finish his psychology studies in Nijmegen and thereafter to enroll in the program of studies in "religion and psychiatry" at the Menninger Institute in Topeka, Kansas.

He took Allport's advice, and from 1964 to 1966 Nouwen studied in Topeka. There he got to know many people who had ideals similar to his own. He became friends with Seward Hiltner, who had laid the groundwork for a new type of pastorate in which psychology was made totally subservient to the practical aspects of theology.[7]

The Menninger Institute was the birthplace of pastoral psychology, and especially for the development of programs for clinical pastoral education (CPE). At present most of the theological programs in the United States and Western Europe have integrated this discipline into their curricula. What is noteworthy is that the student is not occupied with mere theory, but also does practical work in a hospital or a psychiatric institution under direction of a supervisor.[8]

For Nouwen these two years at Menninger were very important. There he discovered and immersed himself in a fruitful combination of subjects (theology and psychology) that were not yet being offered in the Netherlands in any practical sense. The climate of animosity between psychology and theology (psychologists who regard practically every religious expression as a neurosis and theologians who are distrustful of psychology) did not reign at Menninger. On the contrary, Karl Menninger, the

founder of the institute, was a believing Presbyterian, and he let
that play a role in his psychoanalysis. Henri underwent this formation very intensively, creating a fruitful basis for his later life.
He said that there he became spiritually adult. Academic rivalry
was turned into collegial cooperation.

   Slowly Nouwen experienced what it was to become known, to
sojourn among people who were seeking out your qualities. In such
surroundings a person can really thrive. The more theoretical and
dogmatic aspects of belief and theology here assumed a dimension
that Henri later would integrate more and more into his thinking
and acting. What was also very important during this period was
a certain measure of political awakening in Nouwen. The struggle
of Martin Luther King Jr. for Black civil rights brought the United
States into a period of vehement protests. Nouwen participated in
Martin Luther King's great march from Selma to Montgomery in
1965. This affected him deeply. His written account of this march
is very moving and takes us back to those events once again.[9] Little by little he came to know the American spiritual and political
climate. He began to feel at home here. But the idea that he would
stay had not entered the picture as yet. It was his intention to
introduce what he had discovered and learned in Topeka into the
program of religious education in the Netherlands.

Teacher and Fledgling Writer: Topeka and Notre Dame

Even so, the return journey to the Netherlands would have to
wait, for something else turned up. At Menninger Nouwen became friends with John Santos, a Catholic psychologist. Santos
had been invited by the president of the University of Notre Dame
to set up a department of psychology there. None had yet been
established because from the perspective of church and theology
there was still a certain chilly attitude toward psychology during
these years. People thought that psychology was a threat to the
church and faith and would lead people away from belief; Nouwen had experienced precisely the opposite at Menninger. And so
in order to fulfill his task as well as he could, Santos asked for

His Eminence Bernard Cardinal Alfrink (middle) during a visit to Nouwen in Topeka, Kansas (1965).

Teacher in Utrecht, 1970.

the help of his friend Henri Nouwen. Henri accepted and became a teacher at Notre Dame from January 1966 to 1968.[10] Initially he taught courses in general psychology, but something changed along the way when people discovered that Nouwen, although a psychologist, was still a priest first and foremost and especially interested in pastoral care. Many priests worked among the students on the campus. He came into contact with them and brought into their midst the very things that he had discovered were so worthwhile. All sorts of courses sprang up, which developed into classes in pastoral psychology. Those classes became the basis of a number of articles that were compiled in the book *Intimacy* (1).[11] It was Nouwen's first book and the beginning of a long series of publications.

We noted that Nouwen had no plans to settle in the United States. For him Notre Dame was a fine opportunity to gain some expertise and publish his first book. The question of whether to stay at Notre Dame was not at all difficult to answer. He knew that he wanted to return to the Netherlands. *Creative Ministry* (4) records the results of his teaching at Notre Dame. He developed a fine integration of psychology and practical theology, with special attention to the spirituality of the pastor. The three people who influenced him most profoundly at this time were Anton T. Boisen, Seward Hiltner, and Thomas Merton.[12]

During the next few years Nouwen taught in the Netherlands, first at the Amsterdam Joint Pastoral Institute and then at the Catholic Theological Institute of Utrecht (KTHU) as head of the department of behavioral sciences. He lived in the Dijnselburg seminary in Huis ter Heide. During this time two books came out, *With Open Hands* (3) and his book on Thomas Merton, *Thomas Merton: Contemplative Critic* (2).[13] Both were originally written in Dutch. However, in these training courses the same tension existed between psychology and theology. Nouwen did not want to be strictly a psychologist. If he had to, then his preference was for pastoral psychology, but to do this he would have to become a theologian as well. He was advised to break through this impasse by going to study theology in Nijmegen, with the intention of getting his master's degree. In this way the Institute would have a very well educated and experienced psychologist on the faculty as well as someone who could justify his insights theologically. In 1971 he studied theology in Nijmegen and passed his doctoral exams. Yet Nouwen also had the feeling that doing a dissertation in theology was not his first priority. His heart ultimately did not lie on the scholarly side of his field. Where his heart indeed did lie, in the areas that he had written about in the United States, could be pursued only in a very limited way in the Netherlands. Developments there and in all of Western Europe were turning in a direction that Henri was not against, but which he felt were too heavily imbued with the fashions of the times. Should he then return to the United States after all?

– 3 –

FRUITFUL YEARS:
PROFESSOR AT YALE
(1971–81)

Considering the developments in the Netherlands and his own place within them, it was much less difficult for Nouwen to agree to the next invitation from the other side of the Atlantic. It was Colin Williams, dean of the Yale Divinity School, who asked him if he would like to visit Yale. The book *Intimacy* had made an impression on Williams. Nouwen was the man that people needed, he thought. The relationship between ministry and psychology could reach a higher stage of development under his leadership.

When the offer came for a position at Yale, Henri said yes, but it is interesting to hear his conditions. This is where his business and organizational sense came to the fore. He proposed to Yale that he should not be expected to produce a dissertation, nor should the subject be broached in the future. Further, within three years he wanted a permanent appointment and within five years he wanted to become a full professor. Moreover, he stipulated that what he would write would have to meet only his own criteria and not be measured according to some scientific yardstick. Yale accepted all these conditions; apparently Nouwen had become a very desirable commodity. He was to work there from 1971 to 1981.[14]

It is clear that Henri had created enormous freedom for himself by making this arrangement. It was clear to him that the university world with all its rules and requirements can become an enormous shackle that can damage creativity. It was typical of the American entrepreneurial spirit that people did not flinch at making an exception for such a creative spirit. Almost every year another publication appeared from his hand. Yale was a fruitful period for him. All of the spiritual themes that he encountered in literature or discovered in his own life or among his students stood a chance of being featured in his publications. The lists in the archives suggest that Nouwen studied very hard in preparation for his classes. The whole broad terrain of mysticism and spirituality, of psychology and pastoral psychology came under his review. What is surprising, however, is that no dry theological textbook appeared out of all this (he never chose to write such a book); instead, all of his reading passed through the filter of his own experience. Theology, faith, and church are all very nice and you can say a lot about them, but what kind of impact do they have on you, how do they affect you? This personal approach is what made Nouwen such a beloved and widely read author. It's all so familiar: these are the paths that life follows, this is the human journey.

Reaching Out (8) is for me the high point of the ten or eleven books that were written during his Yale period. Nouwen wrote in the acknowledgments that "this book is closer to me than anything I have written" (8:6). In *Reaching Out* Nouwen wrote down everything that he had "on board" at the moment. Since a number of his ideas, feelings, and experiences converge in this book, I would like to explore it in some depth. Here Henri took some of the insights of his previous books to a deeper level. But more importantly, for the first time the writer himself makes an appearance. "During the last few years I have read many studies about spirituality and the spiritual life; I have listened to many lectures, spoken with many spiritual guides and visited many religious communities. I have learned much, but the time has come to realize that neither parents nor teachers nor counselors can do much more than offer a free and friendly place where one has to discover his own lonely way" (8:8).

Indeed, this was the beginning of a new Nouwen. *Reaching*

Out marked a new period, a striking out on a new path. "For a
long time I have been hesitant to write this book, which has such
a personal background" (8:9). Speaking and writing "about" certain experiences became much more a speaking "out of" those
experiences. What he had advocated up to now only in general,
namely, that you can be pastoral only by learning to descend into
your own interior, he now applied directly to himself. It was time
to start printing the negatives (8:11).

On a second level this book describes how most of the spiritual
concepts which have been used up to now have their counter-
parts. This is revealed in the three central paths of the spiritual
life. "Loneliness" can deepen into "solitude" (being interiorly
alone), "hostility" does not have to remain fixed on itself but can
be converted to "hospitality," and the illusions in which people
are entangled can become steps toward fervent prayer. These are
the polarities that Nouwen writes about. We examine and explore
one pole only to make a sort of pendulum movement and end up
in the other. The negative pole is never eliminated. Rather, the life
of faith moves continuously between the two poles. It is this insight into the presence of polarities in human life that makes this
book such exciting reading. Someone who moves along the path
of the spiritual life never actually arrives.

On the first page of the book Nouwen put himself immediately
at risk. "When after many years of adult life I ask myself, 'Where
am I as a Christian?' there are just as many reasons for pessimism
as for optimism. Many of the real struggles of twenty years ago
are still very much alive. I am still searching for inner peace, for
creative relationships with others and for the experience of God,
and neither I nor anyone else has any way of knowing if the small
psychological changes during the past years have made me a more
or a less spiritual man" (8:10). Nevertheless he continues to try
to unravel the secret in the knowledge that the right to judge the
inner way is reserved for God alone.

The pitch that Nouwen attained in *Reaching Out* is high. As a
reader you tend to think that now he's probably said just about
all that he wants to say. What could possibly be left after reaching such a peak? What more can be added to what's already been

said? Nouwen wrestled long and hard with that question. If there was a ready answer, then it did not lie beyond himself but was hidden still deeper within. He decided to pay a visit to these unfamiliar inner frontiers. He asked to become a monk in a Trappist monastery for seven months.

– 4 –

THE IMPLICATIONS OF NOUWEN'S DEPARTURE FOR THE UNITED STATES

The years when Nouwen was beginning to teach and write were extremely tense ones for the church and theology and for society as a whole, especially in Western Europe. I would like to examine this fact in more detail to show that the period when Nouwen left the Netherlands was essential for his further development.

What exactly was going on? The end of the 1960s and beginning of the 1970s were the years when the "great exodus" began to gain momentum. This process of secularization struck with great intensity. Many of the most beloved facets of the faith were blown away in the raging storm. Within the Roman Catholic Church, Vatican II (1962–65) had been undertaken with much fervor, but the answers of this celebrated council were in fact answers to old questions. In that sense the council came too soon, just before the real movement toward secularization had begun.[15] For the new period in which church and society now found themselves, the council's answers were no longer sufficient. Secularization would cause everything to burst apart at the seams. This process had a much greater impact in the Western European context than in North America. It is a very curious phenomenon that the hyper-modern and high-tech United States continued to be very religious and did not share in the experience of de-Christianization and secularization that was occurring in Western Europe.

36

These turbulent developments naturally were also felt in the theological departments in the Netherlands where Nouwen was working. Students as well as faculty breathed in (often unconsciously) the atmosphere described here. Many experienced it as liberating, but others felt that everything they had held sacred had been lost. There followed an enormous polarization within the churches and theological schools. These tensions could also be observed in society as a whole, as was evident in the student uprisings in all the major universities during the 1960s. Paternalism had to be eliminated, in both society and in the church. The imagination had to take charge, and the imagination cannot tolerate authority or institutions.

Nouwen did not feel at home in this restless, destructive atmosphere.[16] Enormous battles were being waged in which personal feuds were not uncommon; it frequently came to blows. This was no time for introspection; the barricades were more important. For example, the internal doubts that many theological students and future ministers were struggling with regarding their call to serve in the much-maligned churches were worked out in public. There was hardly any room for the external (solidarity) to listen to the internal (intimacy), the hidden communion between God and the individual. The latter was exactly what Nouwen had in mind: to explore the unity between the internal and the external and to make *this* the object of reflection. This, he had discovered, was essential for both the individual and society.

But only a few were willing to listen. Questions about the inner life and spirituality fell further and further outside the range of vision. They disappeared on the fringes and would be obscured for many years by the great social issues. All of theology was aimed at these issues! So it is not surprising that Nouwen literally dropped out of the Dutch picture. He became a forgotten son. In the United States, however, he was becoming better known. His book *With Open Hands* (3) marked his departure from Holland. It was as it were his response to the spirit of the times, and today it is as relevant as ever.

Secularization raged for twenty years in the Netherlands and other Western European countries. Now, in the 1990s, on the

"Can you drink this cup?" In the chapel of Yale Divinity School, 1973.

Henri as a young priest during the opening of the Second Vatican Council in 1962 (the third person standing in the right front line).

brink of a new century, the shadow side of this great process of emancipation is being revealed to a startling degree. Modern men and women of the year 2000 have almost limitless capabilities and knowledge, but their loneliness is vast. Like lost and solitary wanderers, they stare out at a silent universe. The positive results of secularization — sweeping away everything that had become so oppressive — have been turned into secular*ism*. A penetrating coldness has settled everywhere, both personally and socially. There is a great need for warmth, for a Source to refresh you, a Source that offers perspective and above all hope at a time when every ideal and social advance seems to have disappeared. Nouwen's books are all about this hope and this Source. And only now, in the final years of this century, are Nouwen's writings finding their way back to the Netherlands and other countries in Western Europe.

When I look back on the last four decades of this century and I read Nouwen's books in that context, I realize that he left Western Europe at a crucial moment. He missed out on the strip mining operation that was carried out on the (supposed) certainties of the church and theology. He escaped having to experience for himself what it meant to plow on bare rock, to watch your parish dwindle, to see your faculty close down, to experience virulent religious indifference on all sides.

This meant that he did not really have to come up with answers to the questions being asked by thoroughly secularized people.[17] In short, he did not have to theologize from point zero as did so many of his colleagues back home. All this gave his work a very positive charge. The heavy, gloomy, oppressive theological questions that were current at the time were absent. This gives Nouwen's books a graceful quality. He did not deny that all these issues existed, but he chose instead to skirt around them in a wide circle. He was always suggesting that his readers look at the other side of things, that for all the shadowy aspects of life there are many shining facets, and that God, at the intersection of light and darkness, has chosen the light. This light, he insisted, is also present at the bottom of every heart.

But for believers who indeed have gone through that valley,

who have felt the depth of God's absence in the marrow of their bones (and I consider myself among them), and for whom even the very existence of God is a cause for daily struggle, there's a flip side to this positive approach: the question is whether Nouwen's writing can also help in spiritual negation, in the eclipse of God, in the great emptiness. In short, do his books also offer material for reflection for "unbelievers," for eternal doubters? I will come back to this again in part 4 on Nouwen's "theology."

– 5 –

A Search for Depth

"Now, while able to see the end of my life cycle as well as its beginning, I realize that I have only one life to live and that it will be a life covering a period of history of which I not only am a part but which I also helped to shape. Now I see that I cannot just point to Dallas, Viet Nam, My Lai and Watergate as the explanation of why my life was different than I had foreseen, but have to search for the roots of these names in the center of my own solitude." (8:35–36)

During the Yale period there are a number of moments that mark the new challenge of Nouwen's search and that we might describe as a further search for depth in his own spiritual life. First of all, he had four long sabbaticals which kept him away from Yale. Second, his mother died. Third, he fixed his attention firmly on Latin America.

From June to December 1974 Nouwen stayed at the Abbey of the Genesee in Piffard, New York. There he wrote his first journal, *The Genesee Diary: Report from a Trappist Monastery* (9); like his later journals it would turn out to be pivotal for his life and work.[18] His experiences in the monastery gradually began pushing him in a direction that he did not yet want to follow. Moreover, after Genesee his writings would begin to take on a still more personal character. "Reflecting on my past three years of work, I realize more and more that it lacked unity. The many things I did during those years seem disjointed, not really relating to each other, not coming from one source" (9:58–59).[19]

41

Under the direction of Abbot John Eudes, Henri submitted to the strict rhythm of the monastery as a kind of "instant monk." This put his life in a different perspective; every aspect of his inner self was screened. His heart came up for examination; in asceticism and detachment his life got a complete going-over by means of painstaking introspection. "Maybe I spoke more about God than with him" (9:xi). This made him decide to "step back" and ask the question that was on his mind when he entered the monastery: "Is there a quiet stream underneath the fluctuating affirmations and rejections of my little world? Is there a still point where my life is anchored and from which I can reach out with hope and courage and confidence?" (9:xii).

Free of all familiar attachments and commitments, he wanted to examine himself, to ask himself who he really was, who God was for him and what God wanted from him. The notes that he kept of this process were selectively compiled in this journal. The notes are divided by months, each with its own motto. His conversations with the abbot, John Eudes, are the thread that runs through the book. This spiritual direction was an essential part of the retreat. The man Nouwen lets himself be known here in his personal search for God and his fellow human beings. He puts himself on the line, vulnerable and honest. In so doing he becomes a mirror in which the reader's own life becomes visible. "Monks go to a monastery to find God. But monks who live in a monastery as if they have found God are not true monks. I came here to come closer to God, but if I ever let myself believe that I am closer to God than anyone else, I would only be fooling myself. We must search for God, but we cannot find God. We can only be found by him."

At the close of this penetrating time he said: "Perhaps the greatest and most hidden illusion of all had been that after seven months of Trappist life I would be a different person, more integrated, more spiritual, more virtuous, more compassionate, more gentle, more joyful, and more understanding." None of this happened "because a monastery is not built to solve problems but to praise the Lord in the midst of them" (9:193). He was to take this pithy sentence from Genesee as his new program. After those seven months his life would never be the same; it was "a most precious memory which keeps unfolding itself in all that I do or plan to do" (9:194).

The clamor of contemporary events resounded at full volume: Vietnam and Nixon, the end of the Greek dictatorship, hunger in North Africa. All of this was taking place while he was in the safe but discerning environment of a religious community, the abbey. In the abbey his dormant longings to live and work in community were further aroused. He wanted "something like this," but different. It would be many years before he would find "something like this" at L'Arche.

From February to August 1979 he spent some time in the Abbey of the Genesee once again. This period resulted not in a journal but a book of prayers, *A Cry for Mercy* (15).

A third sabbatical followed. For Nouwen these "excursions" were extremely important. Just teaching classes in one place was not enough for him. His inner drive to investigate things, his ever-present restlessness, his uncertainty about whether a professorship was really the proper vocation for him, all these impulses of his restless soul brought him to places where he could give free rein to the struggle for depth in his life. In 1976 he became a fellow at the Ecumenical Institute at Collegeville, Minnesota. This period of research resulted in *The Living Reminder* (10).

During a fourth sabbatical in 1978, Nouwen spent five months in Rome as a scholar in residence at the North American College. The lectures that he delivered there were published as *Clowning in Rome: Reflections on Solitude, Celibacy, Prayer, and Contemplation* (11). Rome reminded him of a circus. The dignitaries and politicians looked like lion tamers, trapeze artists, and jugglers. People observed them with astonishment, supermen who could do things that were just too much for us mere human beings. But the clowns, who keep falling down and getting up again, who are always making mistakes with a laugh and a tear, they're on our side. We can relate to them. In the great city of Rome, Nouwen felt a kinship with the clown. Clowns were the simple people who performed between the main attractions. "Clowns are not in the center of the events. They appear between the great acts, fumble

and fall, and make us smile again after the tensions created by
the heroes we came to admire. The clowns don't have it together,
they do not succeed in what they try, they are awkward, out of
balance, and left-handed, but...they are on our side. We respond
to them not with admiration but with sympathy, not with amaze-
ment but with understanding, not with tension but with a smile.
Of the virtuosi we say, 'How can they do it?' Of the clowns we
say, 'They are like us.' The clowns remind us with a tear and a
smile that we share the same human weaknesses" (11:2–3).

Clowning in Rome is a beautiful, intimate book in which the
passage "Prayer and Thought" is especially striking. This section was honored in 1979 with the Journalism Award from the
Catholic Press Association. "To pray, I think, does not mean to
think about God in contrast to thinking about other things, or
to spend time with God instead of spending time with other
people. Rather, it means to think and live in the presence of
God" (11:70). All our actions must have their origin in prayer.
Praying is not an isolated activity; it takes place in the midst of
all the things and the affairs that keep us active. In prayer, a
"self-centered monologue" becomes a "God-centered dialogue"
(11:70–71).

The death of Nouwen's mother in 1978 was a momentous
event in his life. "A mother was dying, her son was praying,
God was present and all was good" (12:18). This death of a
person who had always been so close to him affected him profoundly. In a deeply moving narrative he related her death, his
farewell to his mother, and his consequent rediscovery of hope.
Their correspondence of many years was suddenly ended. All at
once there no longer was that attentive voice on the other side of
the great ocean, no longer that prayer of his mother on his behalf. "A great deal has happened in these weeks, but what will
happen in the months and years ahead will be far more than I can
now understand. I am still waiting, yet already receiving; still hoping, yet already possessing; still wondering, yet already knowing"
(12:61–62).

By writing about all these events Nouwen could get a great deal
off his chest. Writing had become second nature for him over the

years. Whatever was churning around in his head and his heart,
the changes that occurred each day, came to rest on the written
page, and the written words became a source of consolation for
the writer himself. "Meanwhile, I become more and more aware
that for me writing is a very powerful way of concentrating and of
clarifying for myself many thoughts and feelings" (9:103). Every
day he entrusted his intimate companionship with God and his
fellow human beings to patient sheets of paper.

We notice how much Nouwen's books were the results of specific events. They grew out of classes, were assembled from his
journals, were written down on the occasion of a death.

The Yale years were also marked by the growth of a very
strong attraction for Central and South America. This poor and
oppressed continent, only a few hours' flight from the richest
country in the world, was waking up. Indeed, the poor themselves
were waking up. Economic poverty is not fate; it is an organized
condition. And step by step the church was awakening as well.
For centuries this church was (and often still is) an extension of
the powerful who literally possessed everything. Now it was discovering that the poor come first in the Gospel, that God has a
special bond with those who have nothing. These new discoveries
were articulated in liberation theology, and the oppressive dicta-
tors — who had been legitimized by prior theology — came under
strong criticism.

New worlds began to open up for Nouwen. A political-social
interpretation, until then not noticeably present in his life and
work, now began to take shape. His outlook on the church and
politics was being thoroughly radicalized, although he remained
faithful to the "program" he had launched for himself. In 1972
Henri went to Latin America for the first time and took a course
in Spanish there. The developments on the Latin American continent were very unsettling. What was he doing here in this rich
part of the world when there were so many poor people there?
Don't the poor have the place of honor in the Gospel? Isn't being
intensively occupied with one's own spirituality only half the story
if it fails to acknowledge solidarity with the world? Didn't the
contemplation that he learned in the monastery also require the

A restful (and restless) search for God, Genesee Abbey, 1974.

Latin America. With the Osco-Morena family, Lima, Peru, 1982.

action that flowed from this contemplation? Unsettling questions to be sure, especially for a man like Nouwen, who, as we have seen, never hesitated to put himself at risk.

If we take a good look at the books that he wrote during his last years at Yale, we see that gradually Nouwen had reached a saturation point. After the high points of *Reaching Out* (8), *Clowning in Rome* (11), and especially *The Genesee Diary* (9), the other books from that period did not have anything new to offer. In *Making All Things New* (14), written at the end of ten years at Yale ("ten joyful years"), everything is reiterated in a short and concise summary. Just as his stay in the monastery had given depth to his life and work, so now, at the beginning of the 1980s, a new challenge was needed. To remain at Yale would mean too much repetition of the same thoughts and ideas. He needed new impulses to keep his work from degenerating into babbling. There was so much excitement in Latin America, with regard to his own vision of spirituality as well, that he slowly began to wonder whether his vocation lay in Latin America. His departure from Yale drew near as this question became more insistent, demanding a personal answer. Several restless years lay ahead of him. In July 1981 Nouwen made his official break with Yale. He was forty-nine years old. An end had come to an extremely fruitful period in his life.

– 6 –

RESTLESS YEARS: LATIN AMERICA AND HARVARD

"Today I became fifty years old. I am glad that I can cele-brate this birthday in the parish of Ciudad de Dios and with my family in Pamplona Alta. I hope that by concluding here half a century of living, I am perhaps moving toward a new way of living and working in the future." (18:119)

We can almost follow Nouwen step by step in Latin America be-cause once again he began keeping a journal during this period. It was later edited and published under the revealing title *Gracias: A Latin American Journal* (18). What I said about *The Genesee Diary* applies to this book as well. It marked a distinct change in Henri's life. His life had taken on a new dimension: close associ-ation with the poor. At Genesee he had learned to base his life in prayer; now he would learn to live with the poor. And both of these are connected in an extraordinary way. "When we have met our Lord in the silent intimacy of our prayer, then we will also meet him in the *campo,* in the market, and in the town square. But when we have not met him in the center of our own hearts, we cannot expect to meet him in the busyness of our daily lives. Gratitude is God receiving God in and through the human in-teraction of ministry. This viewpoint explains why true ministers, true missionaries, are always also contemplatives. Seeing God in the world and making him visible to each other is the core of ministry as well as the core of the contemplative life" (18:21).

This, in a few key sentences from *Gracias,* is Nouwen in his essence. This is the way he wanted to look at himself and at others. Wherever he might find this duality of action and reflection, struggle and worship, there he would feel at home.

From October 1981 through March 1982 Nouwen stayed in Latin America, beginning with a three-month Spanish course in Cochabamba, Bolivia, at the Instituto de Idiomas of the Maryknoll congregation. He then spent three months in Peru, living with a family in a small house in a poor barrio in Lima. "It is like a monk's cell between a large sea of houses and people" (18:109). The slum had grown up spontaneously as the poor had squatted there and was called Ciudad de Dios, City of God. He had already taken a language course at an earlier point in his life, the summer of 1972, in Bolivia. So the desire to become "a priest for the poor" had very deep roots and had been with him for a long time. The political situation in many countries seemed hopeless. President Ronald Reagan's oppressive administration supported military dictatorships, and Reagan played the Cold War "game" in its most risky and dangerous form by means of an enormous weapons buildup. It was the beginning of the 1980s, and the world was poised on the brink of a third world war. These political facts are reflected in his journal entries. In the midst of these dark developments there was one hope that inspired many. It was the awakening of the cruelly oppressed peoples of Latin America. Liberation theology kept close track of this awakening and provided a voice for the millions of voiceless people. Gustavo Gutiérrez of Lima, Peru, is the father of this theology of liberation. Henri had a great admiration for him and met with him regularly.[20]

Nouwen's spirituality began to take on more socially critical features, something that had not been very pronounced up until then. It was a logical development. Now his nose was pressed up against the undeniable facts. What he had heard and read about at the university was now literally right before his eyes: bitter poverty, uncompromising oppression, and horrible economic

exploitation. Nouwen thus developed a spirituality of social involvement. Whether he would maintain this indefinitely will be
seen later on. "Puebla" (the third general gathering of Latin
American bishops in 1979) was exceptionally stimulating, and
Henri drank it all in. But he continued to remain true to his own
well-developed insights, and as time passed he would not hesitate
to question liberation theology. He was afraid that liberation theology had become too much a thing "of the world," too much
a copy of some other socially critical theory. Nouwen wondered
"if a spirituality of liberation does not need to be deepened by a
spirituality of exile or captivity" (18:40).

The spiritual dimension of liberation theology that Nouwen
advocated did not reach the theological world of Western Europe
during those early years. He often said to me at that time, "You
Western European theologians only pick out the political and
social and ignore the spiritual dimension because it doesn't suit
you." Nouwen saw this unity of prayer and action, reflection and
involvement in Gustavo Gutiérrez more than the other liberation
theologians. "What struck me most was Gustavo's ability to integrate a spirituality of struggle for freedom with a spirituality of
personal growth. He placed great emphasis on the importance of
personal friendship, affective relationships, 'useless' prayer, and
intimate joy as essential elements of a true struggle for liberation"
(18:144–45). Many people simply overlooked this liberation *spirituality*, although it was already present in Gutiérrez's standard
work, *The Theology of Liberation*.[21] Later Gutiérrez would ex-
pand on these insights in *We Drink from Our Own Wells: The
Spiritual Journey of a People*. The affinity between Gutiérrez and
Nouwen was revealed when Nouwen wrote a detailed foreword
to the English edition of this work.[22]

It is also interesting to follow Nouwen's path in his journal
entries in relation to his personal development. In *Gracias* he
continually hovers between two extremes. "Unexpectedly, I am
experiencing a deep depression." He had a "deep-seated feeling
of uselessness" and experienced himself "as a stuttering, superflu-
ous presence" (18:130). A short while later, however, one senses a
certain euphoria. Suddenly he seems to have found his spot; now

he knows what he wants! He describes his ideal as follows: "But how would it be if, in the midst of the very poor, a small group of men and women created a space for people to celebrate God's presence? How would it be if, instead of running in all directions, these men and women could draw others into prayer, silence, reflection, sharing of experiences, and singing God's praise? Maybe it is just a romantic dream, but it is a dream that continues to press itself on me" (18:145).[23]

Nouwen sought out advice about this dream, this form of "pastoral presence" (18:147). It "is slowly presenting itself as a vocation to me" (18:154). But the great restlessness remained. As a reader you are constantly being thrown off guard. Does he want to stay here or not? He fiercely examines this imbalance within himself. "Today, I realized that the question of where to live and what to do is really insignificant compared to the question of how to keep the eyes of my heart focused on the Lord....The difference was never based on the situation itself, but always on my state of mind and heart. When I knew that I was walking with the Lord, I always felt happy and at peace. When I was entangled in my own complaints and emotional needs, I always felt restless and divided" (18:151–52). The initial question asked at the beginning of this book keeps recurring in the journal entries. "Does God call me to live and work in Latin America in the years to come?" (18:xiv).

He ends his journal with a surprisingly positive answer. He wants to bring his dream to Peru and put it into practice. He wants to throw in his lot with the Peruvian church, maintaining links to the United States by means of guest lectureships. Through this he could develop a "reverse mission," the rich learning from the poor (18:188). "Just three days before my return to the United States, an appealing, clear, and convincing vocation has started to take form." Nouwen had the feeling that all was settled. "This, indeed, could become my country, my home, my church, and these people could become my fellow Christians, my friends, and my co-workers in the ministry....I did not feel like a stranger anymore....I felt more like a guest" (18:182–83).

The casual reader who finishes the journal *Gracias* is left with the idea that before too long Nouwen will be a priest in Peru. The last pages tell about his flight back to the United States to take care of a number of essential matters before settling in Peru.

However, those who know Henri better and have read some of his later books realize that things turned out in a totally different way. Latin America was only a short, albeit it very important, episode in Nouwen's life, but it was not the sort of experience that would provide the goal of his vocation. In later books he indicated why it turned out so differently. I will discuss this later on. Even so, it is interesting to examine the pages of *Gracias* itself for the traces of this negative decision.

First of all, I think that Nouwen wanted to settle in much too quickly, although he had often heard from others that many years are needed for that to happen. The second clue has to do with the first. As a Western-educated priest your ideology tells you to give preference to the poor (that's what the liberation theologians say after all), but in practice this can be very disappointing. It certainly must have been difficult for someone like Nouwen, who was so used to providing leadership, making plans, and initiating projects. It isn't easy for such a person to have to play second fiddle. And when the Spanish language does not come very easily on top of everything else, then little is needed for you to abandon such a radical undertaking. Finally there was Henri's attachment to the Western world, a world complete with every convenience and "perfectly" organized, in contrast to Latin America, a world of dust, noise, heat, and discomfort, where almost everything goes wrong and almost nothing happens at the appointed time. Adjusting to such a cultural shock takes years, too many years for the impatient and always restless Nouwen.

What is so fascinating about a writer like Nouwen is that he provides his readers with insight into the various options that presented themselves in his life. He would never have denied the practical arguments that I have put forward here, but he would have tried to explore them at a deeper level. In Nouwen's third lengthy journal, *The Road to Daybreak* (23), he says in retrospect, "I sincerely tried to discern whether living among the poor in Latin America was the direction to go. Slowly and painfully, I discovered that my spiritual ambitions were different from God's will for me. I had to face the fact that I wasn't capable of doing the work of a missioner in a Spanish-speaking country, that I needed more emotional support than my fellow missioners could offer, that the hard struggle for justice often left me discouraged and dispirited, and that the great variety of tasks and obligations took away my inner composure. It was hard to hear my friends say that I could do more for the South in the North than in the South and that my ability to speak and write was more useful among university students than among the poor" (23:3). But this doesn't alter the fact that Nouwen's biography without this Latin American experience would be another story completely. Many years later he said in the foreword to a new edition of *Gracias* that "without the experiences recorded in this journal, I wouldn't be where I am today."[24]

What did he learn and experience then in this period? I have never seen this better expressed than in the earlier mentioned foreword to Gutiérrez's book about humankind's spiritual sources.

"But as I reflect on the impact of this spirituality on my way of living and thinking, I realize that a reductionism has taken place on my side. Talking with those pastoral workers during the summer course, I became aware of how individualistic and elitist my own spirituality had been. It was hard to confess, but true, that in many respects my thinking about the spiritual life had been deeply influenced by my North America milieu with its emphasis upon the 'interior life' and the methods and techniques for developing that life. Only when I confronted what Gustavo calls 'the irruption of the poor into history' did I become aware of how 'spiritualized' my spirituality had become. It had been, in fact, a spirituality for introspective persons who have the luxury of the time and space needed to develop inner harmony and quietude. I had even read the Gospels in a rather romantic way" (xvi).[25]

So in March 1982, Nouwen returned to the United States. In the meantime Harvard had made contact with him. The idea of "reverse mission" appealed to the Harvard Divinity School. Would it not be possible for Nouwen to come to Harvard to teach, they asked. And in such a way that his "live" contacts with Latin America might be fruitful for future ministers. After a time of preparation it was agreed that Nouwen would teach at Harvard for half the year and during the other half he would be free to go wherever he wanted. It was a generous offer from this very prestigious American university. Nouwen would work there for less than three years, from January 1983 until the summer of 1985. The search for a vocation persisted; the restlessness kept gnawing at him. During the second half of 1983 he spent a month in Mexico, and from there he traveled to Nicaragua and Honduras. Back in the United States he gave many lectures to draw the attention of the American people to the terrible oppression in Central America. It became his most politically active period. Later, in his book on the prodigal son, he would look back on this period: "After my long self-exposing journey, the tender embrace of father and son expressed everything I desired at that moment. I was, indeed, the son exhausted from long travels; I wanted to be embraced" (29:4).

From August 27 to September 5, 1984, Nouwen was in Guatemala. When he returned he wrote a moving account of the murdered priest Stanley Rother and Henri's friend John Vesey, who had tried to fill the void there with all the dangers that that entailed. The book is called *Love in a Fearful Land: A Guatemalan Story* (19). It is a book about unwavering trust, tales full of patience, abandonment, working and waiting, not expecting great results. It is about establishing trust by being present in the place where you have been sent. It's enough to make you jealous, Nouwen seems to be saying; if only I could do that — I, the restless soul, who can't come to terms with where I am, I, who have such difficulty living in the here and now.

Then suddenly something happened that would have a deep and profound impact on the rest of Nouwen's life. A meeting that had taken place years before came into startling focus. Harvard would seem like a mere waiting room for something totally different. A major decision was already casting its first shadows.

– 7 –

Home at Last

Once again, a journal marks the transition to a new phase as a third major change took place in Nouwen's life. The title is simple, the content is a frank confession: *The Road to Daybreak: A Spiritual Journey* (23). The foreword to the journal begins thus: "In the late seventies, when I was on the faculty of Yale Divinity School, someone paid me a visit that would radically change my life" (23:1). It was a young woman, Jan Risse, who had come knocking, bringing him greetings from Jean Vanier, the founder of the L'Arche communities. Nothing more, only his greetings. Nouwen had heard of L'Arche and its founder, but beyond that there was no special relationship. During her visit, Jan Risse told him about L'Arche, about the international network of this community, originally French, where mentally handicapped people live together with their assistants. "A few years went by. I had completely forgotten about Jan's visit. Then one morning Jean Vanier called and said: 'I am making a short retreat in Chicago. Would you like to join me?' Again for a moment, I thought he wanted me to give a talk there. But he insisted. 'Henri, it is a *silent* retreat. We can just be together and pray.' Thus Jean and I met. In silence. We spoke a bit, but very little. In the years that followed, I made two visits to his community in France. During my second visit I made a thirty-day retreat and gradually came to the realization that Jan Risse's visit had been the first of a series of events in which Jesus was responding to my prayer to follow him more fully" (23:2).

Farewell to the Academic World

In the fall of 1983 Nouwen made his first visit to Trosly, a village just north of Paris in France, the first community of the L'Arche movement, where Jean Vanier founded the movement with Père Thomas.[26] A new adventure had begun. The following year, in December 1984, he went once again, this time for a thirty-day retreat. A longing began to grow in him to become a part of this community. But what about his professorship at Harvard? How would he deal with that? These were difficult questions for Henri. His internal struggle was intense. "My decision to leave Harvard was a difficult one. For many months I was not sure if I would be following or betraying my vocation by leaving. The outer voices kept saying, 'You can do so much good here. People need you!' The inner voices kept saying, 'What good is it to preach the Gospel to others while losing your own soul?'" (23:22).

Nouwen started his third trimester at Harvard during the first half of 1985. He no longer felt at home there. The environment of this world-famous university with all its constraints and pressures seemed completely opposed to what he had discovered in Latin America and even more at Trosly: life with the poor. The words that he used to typify the vast distance between the two ways of life are "upward mobility" and "downward mobility" (see also chapter 15 below). At Harvard, the pursuit of the higher, greater, more beautiful, more expensive, and richer is an upward spiral that ends in total estrangement. The world of the Gospel is a constant movement downward, to the foundation of society, to the poor. In the faces of the poor (and at Trosly in the faces of the mentally handicapped) appears the face of the Other. Now that the two options could be seen in such clear contrast to each other it became easier to make a decision. Nouwen left Harvard at the end of that trimester. "As soon as I left, I felt so much inner freedom, so much joy and new energy, that I could look back on my former life as a prison in which I had locked myself" (23:22).

Getting to Know L'Arche

A new challenge was beginning, an unfamiliar world was waiting. Would he finally begin to feel at home at L'Arche? Haven't we seen all this before: Nouwen's practice of beginning something with great enthusiasm only to change his mind in the end and take another route? His adventure in Latin America, for example. Wasn't that a leap in the darkness? Hadn't he burned all his bridges behind him?

The skeptic has questions aplenty — the same pragmatic questions that must have been running endlessly through Nouwen's own mind. But he added an even more fundamental question: the question about his own vocation. For the important factor is not only what you yourself want or aspire to; no, the Other is pushing and pulling at the same time. You will be carried off where you do not wish to go! (John 21:18). In chapter 10 I will examine the notion of "vocation," which is a key concept in Nouwen's spirituality.

For Henri the moment had finally arrived to become more intimately acquainted with L'Arche. From August 1985 to August 1986 Nouwen spent a whole year in Trosly. The journal *The Road to Daybreak* (23) provides accompaniment to his new choices.

"My Call Is Being Tested"

Now that Harvard was behind him and he was no longer under such exhausting pressure, Nouwen was able to devote himself wholly to an intensive stay at Trosly. His relationship with Jean Vanier and equally with Père Thomas, the founders of L'Arche, gradually convinced him that this was his long sought-after home. From them he learned that "the poor" are guides for the spiritual life. Up until then Nouwen had had minimal contact with mentally handicapped people, let alone any opportunity to care for them directly. It was a whole new experience for him. In the book *Lifesigns*, which Nouwen wrote during this year, he made a dis-

tinction between being productive and being fruitful. The first is
a dominant factor in the world of the healthy and strong and in
the culture that fosters them, which is aimed at production and
products. In relationships with the handicapped you learn that
the fruit is more important than the product. "Products need constant maintenance in order to prevent breakdown. Fruits, on the
other hand, ask only for the rich soil, water, air, and sunlight
of a caring environment in order to flourish" (20:71). For this
reason he called handicapped people our "healers" (20:72) and
"true barometers of the human spirit" (20:73). The spirituality of
L'Arche fit in very well with his own discoveries, but it also offered a dimension that had been missing up until then: living and
working in a believing community.

From October 1 to 10, 1985, Nouwen made a ten-day visit to
the L'Arche community "Daybreak" in Richmond Hill, a suburb
of Toronto, Canada. At the end of his visit he wrote, "In my nine
days at Daybreak I came to feel intimately a part of the intense
joys and sorrows of this community of care. I have a deep love
for the handicapped men and women and their assistants, who
all received me with such warm hospitality. They did not hide
anything from me. They allowed me to see their fears and their
love. I feel deeply grateful for having been part of it all. I know
that these days will deeply affect not only my time in France but
also my decisions about the years to come" (23:43). The second
interruption came from May 12 to June 23, 1986, when Nouwen
made of a trip around the world (23:207).

On December 12, 1985, an extremely important letter was sent
to Henri from Canada: "We are asking you to consider coming to
live with us in our community of Daybreak.... We truly feel that
you have a gift to bring us" (23:94). This letter moved Nouwen
profoundly because the invitation touched upon the struggle that
he was undergoing in deciding what vocation to follow. "It is the
first time in my life that I have been explicitly called. All my work
as priest since my ordination has been a result of my own initiative. My work at the Menninger Clinic, Notre Dame, Yale, and
Harvard and in Latin America has been work that I myself chose"
(23:95). This calling from beyond himself moved Nouwen deeply.

This time it was not himself but another who took the initiative in his formation.

The rest of his journal shows how his answer to this calling grew within him. Using himself as a model, he shows the many ups and downs that can occur in the search for a human destination. One day the calling may be very clearly perceived; the next day it falls back into the shadows. Is there never a single progression in the human search? Can the seeking individual never find a point of rest? On his fifty-fourth birthday he sighed, "Looking back, I realize that I am still struggling with the same problems I had on the day of my ordination twenty-nine years ago. Notwithstanding my many prayers, my periods of retreat, and the advice from many friends, counselors, and confessors, very little, if anything, has changed with regard to my search for inner unity and peace. I am still the restless, nervous, intense, distracted, and impulse-driven person I was when I set out on this spiritual journey" (23:127). But in spite of these almost unchanging psychological characteristics, he confessed that he had indeed become more intimate with Christ. "Here I feel that something has grown in me. Here I sense that I am not the same person that I was twenty-nine years ago" (23:127).

In July 1986 the year in Trosly ended for Nouwen. He honestly admitted that "Trosly had not become a true home for me" (23:210). Nouwen had become too North American to thrive here. But during that year he had come to know the spirituality of L'Arche at a very deep level, a spirituality in which the mentally handicapped person precedes us in the search for the Source. Those who dare to join this search discover intimacy, fertility, and ecstasy: Remain in me, then you will bear fruit and your joy will be complete (John 15:4ff). Using these three concepts, Nouwen presents what he discovered at Trosly in his book *Lifesigns* (20). The people who inspired him were Jean Vanier and Père Thomas ("the John of the Cross of our time," 23:10), not to mention Pauline Vanier, Jean's mother. He lived in her home in Trosly. This strong, aristocratic, and religious woman made a deep impression on Nouwen as "one of the most vibrant, articulate and spirited people I have ever met" (24:8).[27]

At the end of August 1986, Nouwen became the pastor of the Daybreak community. For this first period he lived and worked with six handicapped people and a number of assistants in one of the houses on the grounds of Daybreak. Adam, a severely handicapped young man, was entrusted to Nouwen's care. Adam taught him to turn a new page in his life. It was "a radical self-confrontation" (23:220) in the midst of a community of people who ultimately were all broken. "And here my deepest handicap appeared" (23:222).

– 8 –

NOUWEN'S THREE JOURNALS:
A BIRD'S-EYE VIEW

Nouwen's three journals are very important "ego" documents, written at the critical moments when equally important decisions were being made. *The Genesee Diary* (9) came at the end of a ten-year period of teaching at Yale. *Gracias* (18) recounted his passion for Latin America and the possibility of staying there. *The Road to Daybreak* (23) described Nouwen's decision to live with mentally handicapped people.

The journals are among Nouwen's most engrossing writings. From day to day we follow his spiritual progress. By bringing his life and his life's choices into dialogue with God, he gives the books their power. And in addition to his own life he includes society as a whole, the church, and theology. Nothing is hidden from Nouwen's searching spirit. Always on the go, always holding his own motives up to the question: "Where does God want me to be?"

This makes the journals little reflections of the age. *The Genesee Diary* showed how an active life within a hyperactive society could run aground, there at the end of the 1960s. *Gracias* focused on the period at the end of the 1970s and beginning of the 1980s. Nouwen did not want merely to pay lip-service to the growing social involvement of those years; he wanted to subject himself to it as well; he actually went to Latin America and he made up his mind to stay there. It was the time of the changing of structures, time for a theology of liberation that could serve as a guide in all this change. In the mid-1980s (in 1984 to be exact) Henri and I

Henri with his housemates at Daybreak, 1992.

first met. But structures are large and tenacious. They can cripple you and make you impatient. No, they can't be changed; things aren't moving fast enough. The rich are firmly implanted in the saddle.

Nouwen carried the interior life at Genesee (the contemplative side) into the fierce active resistance against exploitation in Latin America. Equipped with that interior life he was able to stand firm in the midst of all the troubles, and he believed that that must be the contribution of religion and the church: to nourish humanity's inner life. In Gutiérrez he discovered a kindred spirit, an excellent balance between politics and mysticism. Throughout *Gracias,* however, Nouwen gives you the impression that the active side ruled in many "mission workers," that barricades had taken precedence over the quiet space of the chapel. I think that for this reason Henri became convinced that in the final analysis his vocation did not lie in Latin America. He could keep his "balance" between the inner and the outer life, and he found people there much too inclined toward activism.

That's why the call from Jean Vanier was so important. For the context of L'Arche also included the poor, but these were poor who would remain poor no matter how cut off they were from surrounding structures; they could never overcome their handicaps. This situation really hit home when he realized that the imperfection that exists in this world is something to which he himself and all of us (and *that* is the revelation) are subjected. He learned this inversion/conversion from Jean Vanier, and it fit in perfectly with his lingering doubt about his vocation to Latin America. In fact L'Arche was more difficult, deeper; it profoundly touches the person who really opens himself to it. With the materially poor you can still keep up appearances, but the mentally poor constantly refer you back to yourself. How many times in *The Road to Daybreak* did Nouwen relate that there he could not rely on his books, his wisdom, his reputation? The only things that the main residents of L'Arche asked for were loyalty, nearness, and presence through which they received consolation for their broken lives. And he or she who can give this consolation must be "poor" as well.

Here, indeed, the image of Him who is "pre-eminently Poor" is revealed. In this way interior and exterior lives are linked and forged together; there is no longer any distance between the helper and the person being helped; all the so-called professional tricks are abolished. In this context you learn to reach down to the very foundation of your own existence, and it is the handicapped people themselves who are your teachers. They never stop reminding you of this in a variety of subtle ways. You yourself come into play because the often wordless call of the "poor" wrenches your heart. Through them the Eternal One appears, for God, as one of the poor, is eager to dwell within you — right where you're standing, naked and exposed, eye to eye with your own "inner sanctuary" where the troubled affairs of humanity and society come together and burst apart when the Poor One calls. The encounter with the poor turns out to be an encounter with Jesus. The mystery of the incarnation takes place in the here and now, day after day.

Nouwen's journals provide an account of this spiritual journey that every one of us takes. That which was covered is discovered and rediscovered, the unknown becomes known and recognized, the everyday obligations take on the splendor of an encounter, what is hidden is drawn into the light of revelation. And our world, our history, and within it our own lives are constantly being touched by "eternity." Although we never actually meet the Eternal One, he frequently brushes past us, grazing our temples. Nouwen demonstrated that growth in the spiritual life is possible simply because the way of the Eternal One is an active way and collides with our repeated breakdowns that fall back on well-known remedies. These relapses, which for Nouwen often manifested themselves in periods of stagnation and depression, usually receive more attention in our lives than the quiet growth. The negative scores high in our culture and has media market value. But God travels in God's own unprecedented way, always looking for fertile ground as well as fruitful fields in human life.[28] There God settles, very small and fragile, but still present. This quiet growth, not very interesting for zooming cameras, comes to life where people are healed and have the chance to come to their senses: at L'Arche, Taizé, the Emmaus movement of Abbé Pierre, the list goes on. It doesn't reveal itself right away, but it plants itself like the seeds of something new, in places where the New, the Firstborn, has chosen to make its home, in our midst, like the break of a new day.

– 9 –

MATURING YEARS:
1986 TO HIS DEATH IN 1996

The first years at Daybreak were certainly not easy for Nouwen. He had to make a lot of adjustments to his new situation. There was his unfamiliarity with pastoral care for mentally handicapped people and the newness of living in community. When you are so used to living your own life, it isn't easy to make accommodations to the slow rhythm of the community, to the young age of the volunteer assistants who came together from many countries and had not left their problems at home. New relationships develop with colleagues and with the permanent staff members of Daybreak, and naturally you've got yourself to contend with and everything you've dragged along with you.

Besides being a pastor Henri also continued as a writer, with the emphasis on "also." For direct pastoral work came first and writing had to take place during his scarce free time and the shorter or longer periods that he spent elsewhere. Whenever his writing was driven into a corner Nouwen became restless, so it was very important for him to find a good balance between working and writing. It was a matter of trading off one source of productivity for another. And whoever writes is also asked to come and speak, to lecture, to attend congresses and seminars, to preside at meetings, and so on, not only in North America but also around the world. Indeed, Nouwen's books have been translated into dozens of languages, including Chinese and Japanese. Once when I was a guest at Daybreak, in May 1994, I could see for myself how difficult it was for him to say no to the many invitations, to say nothing of the dozens of letters that arrived each day from his readers. Nouwen tried as much as possible to respond personally, and it was an intense ministry-by-letter. But naturally an end had to come to such efforts. Luckily he had a good secretary with excellent skills who took a lot of work off his hands.

Nouwen hadn't been at Daybreak for a year when he fell into a deep crisis. I will come back to this in chapter 10 when I discuss "vocation." It took a great deal of energy to crawl out of this low point, but thanks to some good help he succeeded. A few years later, in 1989, he was involved in a serious accident. It seemed that narrowly escaping death taught him a valuable lesson. In chapter 14, "Beyond Death," I will take a look at this experience.

His productivity during those years in terms of books was enormous. "Home at last" at Daybreak certainly did not mean sitting still. I count eleven titles, all written in the context of working and living in this vulnerable community. In my estimation his best book is *The Return of the Prodigal Son* (29). It is his most mature work. Whoever produces these kinds of reflections, who is able to write this way at all, must have passed through very hard times and ascended to great heights himself. Nouwen's spiritual journey and his insights into Christian spirituality reach a high point here. In *The Return of the Prodigal Son,* he does not focus on only one aspect of spirituality as he had in many of his other books, but rather he deals with a total spiritual vision, with the eventual completion of a human life in the face of the Eternal One. I will come back to this book again in further discussions.

Nouwen also very much wanted to keep on traveling. The invitations that he did accept took him all over the world. Often he jumped at the chance to make these journeys in order to propagate the ideas behind L'Arche. In July 1993 he was in the Ukraine, where care for the handicapped had only just begun and where people were trying to learn anew about human community and community spirit in the chaos of an almost bankrupt country. "More than ever, I believe in the gift of handicapped people to create such a community. Their weakness is God's strength; their dependence is God's invitation to create bonds of love and support; their poverty is one of God's ways to bring us the blessings of the Kingdom."[29]

All that traveling provided Nouwen with a network of friends and good acquaintances, and it gave him great joy and satisfaction. "Friendship" is a word that was fraught with meaning for Nouwen, and in different places he puts this into words. "Friendship has always belonged to the core of my spiritual journey" (19:91). "Deep friendship is a calling forth of each other's chosenness and a mutual affirmation of being precious in God's eyes" (28:54).[30]

Flying and Catching

Before we move on to the second part of this book, which deals with a number of basic spiritual concepts in Nouwen's work, I want to briefly mention a passion of his final years: the circus, or better, the circus trapeze artists. Time and time again he had insisted that spiritual themes are there for the taking: just look around carefully, go after them, and let them grab you! Spirituality is not the sole property of the church or theology. Wherever people are, there "the Mystery" emerges. At the very most the church and theology can indicate what this Mystery is within, among, and between human beings.

During a vacation in Germany in 1991 Nouwen went with his father to a circus in Freiburg. He was deeply impressed by the South African trapeze artists known as "The Flying Rodleighs." Perhaps "impressed" is a bit too cool an expression: he was thoroughly entranced by them! Before his very eyes he saw all of human life marching by in the persons of those trapeze artists. He was determined to get to know them. Their lives, their profession, their discipline, the "game" they play with their bodies, their fears, the thrill, the honor, the applause, the mistakes, Nouwen made it his business to learn all about these aspects of their work as his friendship developed in the following years with the men and women of this troupe. He watched them, listened to their stories, learned to understand their techniques, and studied the movements of their bodies. He even arranged to travel with the circus in a camper for a time.

For Nouwen the trapeze "story" gradually became a metaphor for the hazardous enterprise called life. The young and well-trained bodies of these artists seemed like the exact opposite of the broken bodies of the handicapped people of Daybreak. Both told a story with their bodies, a story of falling and getting up again, of flying and being caught, of death and resurrection. None of the circus people went with him one Sunday when he visited a church not far from the circus tent. "No one from the circus was there. The circus tent and the church, standing a few hundred feet apart, are two completely separate worlds. For me however, they are connected, but no one seems to see this."[31]

I had hoped that Nouwen would work at combining these themes of spirituality and the physical body. In our "fitness" culture marked by a striving for a certain degree of immortality, it is bitterly necessary that spiritual attention be paid to the body, including the relationship between mysticism and the erotic. Do we not say in the Eucharist, "Take and eat, this is my body"? In his book *With Burning Hearts: A Meditation on the Eucharistic Life* (32), this reality of the physical body is not yet dealt with. But it did come up when he spoke at a major conference on AIDS. He confessed that the body is "sort of a scary thing for me to talk about," but also that he had learned during that conference that the body is not only an image, a metaphor. "I know that I have to discover what it really means to be a body, to be in a body, to be incarnate. I need to learn to be at home in myself, a temple of the Holy Spirit, and therefore fully intimate with God, at home in my home where God dwells."[32]

I had hoped that Nouwen's great wish could be fulfilled, that he would write a story in which these spiritual themes were implicitly present, a kind of novella, perhaps a novel. For that was what occupied his mind during those last few years, a narrative spirituality in which the great words of the Christian tradition could be told in story fashion. *The Return of the Prodigal Son* can be seen as the first attempt, with the stories of Rembrandt and the prodigal son as a starting point. When I finished this book, the book about the circus had not yet appeared, although there had been journal entries about his meetings with the Rodleighs, a television film, and here and there short references to flying and being caught. "One day, I was sitting with Rodleigh, the leader of the troupe, in his caravan, talking about flying. He said, 'As a flyer, I must have complete trust in my catcher. The public might think that I am the great star of the trapeze, but the real star is Joe, my catcher. He has to be there for me with split-second precision and grab me out of the air as I come to him in the long jump.'

"'How does it work?' I asked.

"'The secret,' Rodleigh said, 'is that the flyer does nothing and the catcher does everything. When I fly to Joe, I have simply to stretch out my arms and hands and wait for him to catch me and pull me safely over the apron behind the catchbar.'

"'You do nothing!' I said, surprised.

"'Nothing,' Rodleigh repeated. 'The worst thing the flyer can do is to try to catch the catcher. I am not supposed to catch Joe. It's Joe's task to catch me. If I grabbed Joe's wrists, I might break them, or he might break mine, and that would be the end of both of us. A flyer must fly, and a catcher must catch, and the flyer must trust, with outstretched arms, that his catcher will be there for him'" (31:66–67).

Part 2

THE SPIRITUALITY
OF HENRI NOUWEN:
BASIC THEMES AND
KEY CONCEPTS

– 10 –

VOCATION

Where Are You?

A person is called. It's a call that echoes from the very first pages of the Bible: "Adam, man, where are you?" (Gen. 3:9). Where are you hiding, what are you doing? Man, woman, child, in the midst of all the voices in your lives that are demanding your attention, can't you hear something else, *Someone* else? Sure life is complicated, and it's hard enough just to hold your head above water. A house, a roof over your head, a job, your salary, your vacation, your family, your friends. Do these things keep you so preoccupied that they become the be-all and end-all, or do they help you to find your purpose in life? Purpose — vocation — roughly means finding the very specific place (in you, around you) to which you are being called so that you can be completely yourself, can become whole, can be the very best that you are capable of being. Being called also suggests a movement from somewhere outside you. It is the active passivity involved in rendering yourself open, of listening to the active Presence that is calling you. Vocation assumes a desire to encounter, to approach, to arrive at the spot where the holy joins in the often-ominous course of human life.

Nouwen's books are permeated with this longing for an encounter. They set readers on a trail, encouraging them to examine themselves, to see exactly where they are on their particular path, whether there are any prospects in sight or whether it's just a dead end, to figure out where it is that they should be searching and how to recognize the One who calls. Nouwen's writing is not abstract or pedantic. We could never have gotten to know him so well if his writing had been abstract. No, in a completely unique way he shows how a calling, a vocation, has always played a central role in his own life. A vocation is the hub of one's spiritual life. If there is noise and disturbance between the One Who calls and the one who is called, then the spiritual life gets thrown off balance. There's a great deal of noise and disturbance in every life by definition, and whose life is ever completely balanced?

In his book *Aging*, Nouwen uses the picture of a wagon wheel with a hub in the middle around which literally everything turns. "Although we have only one life cycle to live, although it is only a small part of human history which we will cover, to do this gracefully and carefully is our greatest vocation" (6:14).

Called to Celebrate Life

A vocation is not something that concerns only certain people or certain groups, but that's the way it is often regarded. Most people reserve the idea of vocation to a "spiritual profession," that of a priest, minister, monk, or religious. But according to this point of view a doctor, a lawyer, or a mayor is also more or less called. A vocation makes you different.

Nouwen also talks about vocation in this context, particularly in his first book, which is strongly pastoral and psychological and is directed toward future priests. For example, he discusses the difficulties that a seminary student may have with his vocation, asking himself over and over again "if he should give the most explicit unchangeable commitment to the most undefined and unclear profession. At the same time he wonders who is calling whom" (1:83).

In *Creative Ministry* (4) Nouwen emphasizes that ministers who take a purely professional approach to their work and merely practice a "profession" ultimately deny "the Best" to the people for whom they are working and ruthlessly sell themselves

Henri with his housemates at Daybreak, 1992.

short. What is so special about the vocation of ministers is that they are expected to introduce depth into human lives; they let the beckoning voice of the Other resound in the midst of all the other voices that tempt and seduce. The only ministers who are successful in this work are those who are also willing to put themselves at risk, those who come out from under their own professional skills (of exegesis, dogma, ethics, etc.) and who dare to surrender themselves.

Nouwen's book is still extremely relevant, for there is and generally has been far too little attention paid to the personal spirituality of the minister. The minister "is the man [Nouwen's language was not yet inclusive in those days, but that would change] who challenges us to *celebrate* life; that is, to turn away from fatalism and despair and to make our discovery that we have but one life to live into an ongoing recognition of God's work with man. But how can this celebration really be a human possibility? Our lives vibrate between two darknesses. We hesitantly come forth out of the darkness of birth and slowly vanish into the darkness of death. We move from dust to dust, from unknown to unknown, from mystery to mystery. We try to keep a vital balance on the thin rope that is stretched between two definitive endings we have never seen or understood. We are surrounded by the reality of the unseen, which fills every part of our life with a moment of terror but at the same time holds the secret mystery of our being alive. The Christian minister is the one whose vocation is to make it possible for man not only to fully face his human situation but also to celebrate it in all its awesome reality" (4:90–91).

Thus each profession, and every individual in the final analysis, has a special calling, and the relationships within which people function have a very specific purpose. Marriage, for example. "Marriage is not a lifelong attraction of two individuals to each other, but a call for two people to witness together to God's love. The basis of marriage is not mutual affection, or feelings, or emotions and passions that we associate with love, but a vocation, a being elected to build together a house for God in this world." (11:46).[33]

Vocation or Career?

To crystallize the definition of a vocation in the name of God, Nouwen makes a distinction between vocation and career. These two are not necessarily mutually exclusive, but in a world where career fever and career planning are so highly valued, the element of vocation gets pushed into a corner and people are manipulated into doing things that comply with the social system. The very human freedom that is accentuated in the concept of vocation then disappears. "The word *vocation* comes from the Latin *vocare* which means 'to call.' God calls us together into one people fashioned in the image of Christ. It is by Christ's vocation that we are gathered. Here we need to distinguish carefully between vocation and career.... As soon as we think that our careers *are* our vocation, we are in danger of returning to the ordinary and proper places governed by human competition and of using our talents more to separate ourselves from others than to unite ourselves with them in a common life. A career disconnected from a vocation divides; a career that expresses obedience to our vocation is the concrete way of making our unique talents available to the community" (16:83).

Who Calls Us, and to What Purpose?

Christ himself exemplifies the nature of vocation. He has gone "the way of all flesh" in creative obedience. His uniqueness lies in this: that he is the only One who has followed the voice of his Father with all the consequences that involves, even death! We hit upon the heart of Nouwen's theology when he writes, "God is always active in our lives. He always calls, he always asks us to take up our crosses and follow him. But do we see, feel, and recognize God's call, or do we keep waiting for that illusory moment when it will really happen? ... We do not have to go after crosses, but we have to take up the crosses that have been ours all along. To follow Jesus, therefore, means first and foremost to discover in our daily lives God's unique vocation for us" (16:73).

Nouwen's Own Approach to Vocation

In the biographical part of this book we learned about Nouwen's restless way of life. "Where does God want me to be?" is a question that shimmers behind all his written words. The idea of regarding his own personal vocation as a valuable starting point for the spiritual life grew stronger in him during his periods in the monastery. With the help of the abbot John Eudes he learned to listen to the Voice that sounded in himself and every person, to make a distinction between the authenticity of this Voice and the noise and disturbance that everyday life adds to it, which makes it seem as though the Voice has fallen silent. During one of the last days in Genesee, Nouwen more or less sums it up with the words, "I tried to formulate how I had come to see my own vocation more clearly during this retreat. Two things seem central: I am a priest and I am called to study and teach in the field of Christian Spirituality. Since I was six years old I have wanted to be a priest, a desire that never wavered except for the few moments when I was overly impressed by the uniform of a sea captain. Ever since my studies for the priesthood I have felt especially attracted to what was then called, 'Ascetical and Mystical Theology,' and all my other studies in psychology, sociology, and similar fields never seemed fruitful for me unless they led me to a deeper understanding of the questions of the spiritual life. I have always moved from the psychological to the theological level and from clinical considerations to spiritual concerns. A sequence of courses... seems to illustrate the movement of which I have always been part. Where should the emphasis be now? It seems that my retreat has affirmed and deepened an already existing trend" (9:182).

But just when you think that Nouwen will probably continue following the way of thinking that he has chosen, he swerves once more to the other side. He never denies the existence of a certain insight into the process of his own vocation, even of a measure of spiritual growth, but Nouwen's spirituality is never complete. Translating one's spiritual life in terms of social existence was always an open matter for him, a future full of promise. This gives his work a kind of elegance. It is highly accessible; nothing is fixed and rigid. Sometimes he even seems to consciously undermine the very insights that he has acquired. For example, although well settled at Yale, he looks back on the seven months at Genesee and, as we have seen, writes in the epilogue, "Perhaps the greatest and most hidden illusion of all has been that after seven months of Trappist life I would be a different person, more integrated, more spiritual, more virtuous, more compassionate, more gentle, more joyful, and more understanding... [but] a monastery is not built to solve problems but to praise the Lord in the midst of them" (9:193). You might say that this is how the human vocation is tested and tries to be fully lived in the here and now of everyday life. Nouwen was never one to avoid worldly contact, nor was he eager to fly to some heavenly abode.

The same tests of his vocation were apparent in Nouwen's Latin American "adventure." At the end of *Gracias* (18) he comes to a final decision: his vocation is here! Arriving home he literally makes a 360-degree turn. No, he admits, my vocation is not here. He is driven on relentlessly, always searching for that place where the compass needle points most insistently. First here, then there. Who am I? Where does God want me to be? Where can I be all that I am capable of being? Nouwen's advantage in all of this was a great measure of mobility. He *could* go where he wanted to go; he had the means to do so and he was given the freedom to set out.

Being Called Home

After a great deal of wandering and brooding, L'Arche became the place where Nouwen experienced his vocation most intensively. He speaks about it in terms of coming home, like the prodigal son in the parable. "I was, indeed, the son exhausted from long travels; I wanted to be embraced.... The son-come-home was all I was and all I wanted to be.... I desired only to rest safely in a place where I could feel a sense of belonging, a place where I could feel at home" (29:4–5). Nouwen's calling to L'Arche was a "story of homecoming" — home at last! But wasn't this a bit

euphoric? Was it possible to corral such a lively spirit as Nouwen's? Those who were close to him at that time feared for the
worst, that perhaps he was chasing a shadow, that what he saw
as his vocation was really an escape. When Nouwen entered a
deep crisis during the first year at Daybreak (1986), his friends'
opinions seemed confirmed. "But then, physical and emotional
exhaustion forced me to take a long time off" (24:12). "These
years at Daybreak have not been easy. There has been much inner
struggle, and there has been mental, emotional, and spiritual pain.
Nothing, absolutely nothing, had about it the quality of having
arrived" (29:12).

Nouwen did not reveal very much in his books about the reasons for this deep depression, which forced him to stay for a time
elsewhere in Canada. We know only that it was very intense and
that he interpreted this experience, which seemed to cut him to
the quick, as grace-filled, that is to say, as a defining moment
for his vocation.[34] Happily, "God himself showed me the way.
The emotional and physical crises that interrupted my busy life at
Daybreak, compelled me — with violent force — to return home
and to look for God where God can be found — in my own inner
sanctuary" (29:15). We had never before heard Nouwen speak
so straightforwardly about his vocation. Obviously this was also
something new for him. "I have a new vocation now" (29:15).

His guide in searching for and discovering this new vocation
was Rembrandt, or more precisely, Rembrandt's majestic painting
of the parable of the prodigal son. Nouwen wrote his best book
on this seventeenth-century Dutch painter. It's all here, absolutely
everything that touched him deeply. He holds his own life up to
that of the three(!) main figures in the parable, and Rembrandt's
play of light and darkness adds a magnificent extra element to the
exegesis. Here indeed is another example of a human being being
called to come out of the darkness into the light, to let himself
be touched by the healing hands of the Father, "and claim the
truth with the inner freedom of the child of God." And in the
parable that child is above all the younger son. It is Nouwen himself in his "outer waywardness," the one who finally comes home
and finds a place at L'Arche after numerous wanderings. But he

also is literally the older son, embittered in "inner waywardness," who could have everything of the Father but was not joyful and refused to come into the light. Surprisingly new in this book, however, was Nouwen's description of his vocation to become a father. We had not read that anywhere up to now. "But Rembrandt, who showed me the Father in utmost vulnerability, made me come to the awareness that my final vocation is indeed to become like the Father and to live out his divine compassion in my daily life. Though I am both the younger son and the elder son, I am not to remain them, but to become the Father." (29:114).[35]

Called to Serve

Mysticism and ethics have their meeting point in the person of Father/Mother, for the ultimate vocation of a human being is to be there for others. When you are really called by name, you realize that you yourself are the instrument through which the One is active, that the healing hands of God are translated into your healing hands. Just being there, without questions, without demands, emptying yourself so that others can be filled and can be all that they are capable of being. This vocation indeed requires you to pass through the younger and the older sons and to find in yourself the place where God desires to dwell.

This was a new discovery for Nouwen: *that* was his new vocation. He says, "For many years I tried to get a glimpse of God by looking carefully at the varieties of human experience: loneliness and love, sorrow and joy, resentment and gratitude, war and peace. I sought to understand the ups and downs of the human soul, to discern there a hunger and thirst that only a God whose name is Love could satisfy. I tried to discover the lasting beyond the passing, the eternal beyond the temporal, the perfect love beyond all paralyzing fears, and the divine compassion beyond the desolation of human anguish and agony. I tried constantly to point beyond the mortal quality of our existence to a presence larger, deeper, wider, and more beautiful than we can imagine, and to speak about that presence as a presence that can already

now be seen, heard, and touched by those who are willing to believe. However, during my time here at Daybreak, I have been
led to an inner place where I had not been before. It is the place
within me where God has chosen to dwell. It is the place where
I am held safe in the embrace of an all-loving Father who calls
me by name and says, 'You are my beloved son, on you my favor
rests' " (29:14).

Vocation and Inevitable Loneliness

It is because of this sojourn of the Eternal One in our deepest interior that we are able to become spiritual fathers and mothers.
Therein lies our vocation, which we carry out in grief, forgiveness, and generosity (29:120). This vocation is both heavy and
light, heavy because it goes hand in hand with great loneliness.
Indeed, who has the task of waiting patiently for the homecoming
of God's wounded human children in order then to bless them? It
is "the loneliness of the Father, the loneliness of God, the ultimate
loneliness of compassion" (29:128). It is born of the "dread-
ful emptiness in this spiritual fatherhood" (29:124). That's why
there's always resistance to this vocation as well as the realization
that there's no escaping it. "I see clearly the truth of my vocation
to be a father; at the same time it seems to me almost impossible to follow it" (29:128). Is it possible to live out this vocation,
given its heaviness? Or do we first have to experience its heaviness
in order to discover its other light, joyful side? "Father" Nouwen ("on the basis of my priestly ordination am I spoken of in
this way") responds: "But who is going to be home when they
[the handicapped and all the others] return — tired, exhausted,
excited, disappointed, guilty, or ashamed? Who is going to convince them that, after all is said and done, there is a safe place to
return to and receive an embrace? If it is not I, who is it going
to be? The joy of fatherhood is vastly different from the pleasure
of wayward children.[36] It is a joy beyond rejection and loneliness;
yes, even beyond affirmation and community. It is the joy of a
fatherhood that takes its name from the heavenly Father and par-

takes in his divine solitude. It does not surprise me at all that few people claim fatherhood for themselves. The pains are too obvious, the joys too hidden. And still, by not claiming it I shirk my responsibility as a spiritually adult person. Yes, I even betray my vocation" (29:129).

This last paragraph almost automatically brings us to another important key concept in Nouwen's spirituality, the theme of solitude.

– 11 –

SOLITUDE

The Lonely Landscape

Following our own vocation and listening to the inner voice brings us to a place that we had not known about until now. We have begun believing in the voice that calls us, and this gives us the courage to continue on our way. But the first contours that we see in this new landscape point to barrenness, desolation, and inconsolable solitude. What have we undertaken? We're tempted to make a U-turn, but is there a way back? Isn't this really typical whenever you reluctantly set out on the *one* path that you *must* travel? You might just as well say, "Today I'm ten years younger," as to say, "That's it, I'm not going." In the entire body of spiritual and mystical literature, sooner or later we run up against the crunching sound of solitude, and Nouwen is no exception. It sounds like snow under your feet on a cold, quiet winter night. For under the surface of daily life, rough streams are seething and swirling, threatening to knock you down and take your life. And like a smoldering fire they flare up in unexpected moments.

Nouwen is a good guide for exploring this lonely landscape. He deals with both personal and social loneliness. Nowhere does he play the personal against the political and social, but he frequently emphasizes the interconnection between the two. "Ultimately, I believe that what is most personal is also the most universal" (3:7).

The Solitary Desert

In order to show what Nouwen meant by solitude, I will quote a passage in which he says what solitude is *not*.[37] "In order to understand the meaning of solitude, we must first unmask the ways in which the idea of solitude has been distorted by our world. We say to each other that we need some solitude in our lives. What we really are thinking of, however, is a time and a place for ourselves in which we are not bothered by other people, can think our own thoughts, express our own complaints, and do our own thing, whatever it may be. For us, solitude most often means privacy. We have come to the dubious conviction that we all have a right to privacy. Solitude thus becomes like a spiritual property for which we can compete on the free market of spiritual goods. But there is more. We also think of solitude as a station where we can recharge our batteries, or as the corner of the boxing ring where our wounds are oiled, our muscles massaged, and our courage restored by fitting slogans. In short, we think of solitude as a place where we gather new strength to continue the ongoing competition in life. But that is not the solitude of St. John the Baptist, or St. Anthony or St. Benedict, of Charles de Foucauld or the brothers of Taizé. For them solitude is not a private therapeutic place. Rather, it is the place of conversion, the place where the old self dies and the new self is born, the place where the emergence of the new man and the new woman occurs" (13:26–27). In the last sentence Nouwen in fact does say what solitude is: it's a process, a way for us to descend into ourselves, an inner search. There, in the desert of the individual heart, a conversion slowly takes place, at least if we do not run away from the many tempters and confusers (*diabolos,* devil).

In Nouwen's book on the desert fathers, we see that this is precisely why these mystics of the first and second centuries went into the desert: to do battle with their own demons, demons which were and still are brutally tyrannizing society — greed, ambition, pressure to achieve, and so on. "That is the struggle. It is the struggle to die to the false self" (13:28). Only then is there space for social involvement; ethics follows conversion. If we do not wait for conversion, then our approach to humanity can run into the danger of becoming a battle against our own frustrations and irritations. "St. Anthony spent twenty years in isolation. When he left it he took his solitude with him and shared it with all who came to him. Those who saw him described him as balanced, gentle, and caring. He had become so Christlike, so radiant with God's love, that his entire being was ministry" (13:32).

Loneliness and Solitude

Solitude is a necessary but at the same time a never-ending phase as we search for ourselves, for God, and for our neighbor. "When you are able to create a lonely place in the middle of your actions and concerns, your successes and failures slowly can lose some of their power over you" (7:26). Even if you go through the depths of abandonment, there, far away in the depths of your own heart and in the heart of the world, Someone awaits you. In Nouwen spirituality always takes on a christological intensity. By looking at Jesus' life we learn how all our lives are actually and intrinsically put together. The difference between him and us is that he alone followed his vocation into the deepest solitude.

We saw that solitude is not the same as the human desire for isolation and privacy, nor is it purely a psychological process for becoming a fully integrated person. No, human solitude reveals that there is an Other who directs our lives, who has plans for us, who wants happiness and salvation for this world.

In order to bring this spiritual solitude into sharper focus, Nouwen makes a distinction between two kinds of solitude. In English this is better distinguished than in Dutch, where "loneliness" is translated as *eenzaamheid* and "solitude" as *alleen zijn*. The first, loneliness, is a concept full of negativity, but solitude should be understood as a very positive spiritual concept. All too often, solitude lies hidden behind, under, or within loneliness.

In the first part of his book *Reaching Out* (8) Nouwen deals extensively with the difference and the relationship between these two concepts. He sees loneliness as the single greatest malady of modern times. "Loneliness is one of the most universal sources of human suffering today.... The roots of loneliness are very deep and cannot be touched by optimistic advertisement, substitute love-images or social togetherness" (8:15–16). And next comes something that is extraordinarily important to understanding Nouwen's spirituality. For instead of descending into the dark hole of this stifling loneliness, we human beings are inclined to run away from it. Instead of seeing the great malady of our society, which is crushing so many people, as a challenge to change (in order to make society more humane), we continue to develop defense mechanisms and surrogate images. More luxuries, more possessions, higher, better, it's never enough. The advertising industry displays this artificial and deceptive world better than anyone else. "In our emergency-oriented world, fear and anger have become powerful forces in human behavior" (11:11). Evening after evening we are told that we can escape this human defect, loneliness, that there's a kind of medicine we can take for it, so to speak. "All around us we see the many ways by which the people of the western world are trying to escape this loneliness. Psychotherapy, the many institutes which offer group experiences with verbal and nonverbal communication techniques, summer courses and conferences supported by scholars, trainers and 'huggers' where people can share common problems, and the many experiments which seek to create intimate liturgies where peace is not only announced but also felt — these increasingly popular phenomena are all signs of a painful attempt to break through the immobilizing wall of loneliness" (5:83–84).

Solitude as Gift

In such a situation, absolutely everything is expected from neighbor, friend, partner, or family member. Okay, our fellow human beings can help us in our loneliness, but our solitude is something we have to sort out ourselves; it's everyone's spiritual journey. In almost all of his books, Nouwen warns against the illusion that those around us can eliminate our solitude. "When our loneliness drives us away from ourselves into the arms of our companions in life, we are, in fact, driving ourselves into excruciating relationships, tiring friendships and suffocating embraces.... No friend or lover, no husband or wife, no community or commune will be able to put to rest our deepest cravings for unity and wholeness" (8:19).

But then what are we to do? Nouwen proposes that the only clear path is also the most difficult, for the "gods" of gold and gain, of pleasure and splendor, always play a very strong role in our lives. "This difficult road is the road of conversion, the conversion from loneliness into solitude. Instead of running away from our loneliness and trying to forget or deny it, we have to protect it and turn it into a fruitful solitude. To live a spiritual life we must first find the courage to enter into the desert of our loneliness and to change it by gentle and persistent efforts into a garden of solitude" (8:22).[38] Here is where Nouwen locates much of the tragedy in human relationships. We think that another human being can give us what no person *can* give. No one, no matter how close or beloved he or she is, can enter into that existential lonely spot in our interior life. To put it more strongly, expecting and desiring such from another does violence to our relationship. For when the person in question comes up short in meeting this need, something that he or she will inevitably do, then rage and blame are just around the corner.

In his lectures, Nouwen often used an image of our two hands; when we interlock our fingers so that our hands are clasping each other they become solid and unyielding. That's not how relationships should be. It would be much better if both hands (both people in a relationship) were just touching at the fingertips and pointing upward, so that it becomes evident that there's a Third Person involved. This creates space and allows for creativity so that people aren't completely wrapped up in each other, so they don't expect too much of each another, but instead are able to play the game of love in freedom.

With this spiritual vision of human relationships Nouwen was taking a stand against the dominant psychological approach of our times. He did not want to suppress existential human loneliness, but in the final analysis he wanted to see it as a source for every life, a Source where Love dwells. "The Christian way of life does not take away our loneliness; it protects and cherishes it as a precious gift" (5:84). The paradox "the closer you are to yourself, the closer you are to the other" is a piece of spiritual wisdom in Nouwen's thought because it draws its sources of energy from elsewhere. "Solitude indeed is the place of the great encounter, from which all other encounters derive their meaning" (11:28).[39]

Traveling the human path via the apparent detour of one's own inner solitude brings people together. Indeed, each of us possesses the same solitude and for each of us the same encounter takes place. It is an encounter with God, the One who is eager to meet us, who binds everyone together in this encounter. "In real solitude there is an unlimited space for others, because there we are empty and there we can see that, in fact, nobody stands over and against us" (11:31). Brotherhood and sisterhood, humanity and involvement, these are found within and at the basis of this encounter in solitude "because solitude is the place where God reveals himself as God-with-us, as the God who is our creator, redeemer, and sanctifier, as the God who is the source, the center and purpose of our existence....In solitude, we meet God. In solitude, we leave behind our many activities, concerns, plans and projects, opinions and convictions, and enter into the presence of our loving God, naked, vulnerable, open, and receptive" (11:27–28).

Not long after Nouwen's death, his book *Bread for the Journey: A Daybook of Wisdom and Faith* (36) appeared. This work contains short, meditative reflections for every day of the year. Nowhere else have I seen the ideas contained in this chapter so fully expressed. "All human beings are alone. No other person will completely feel like we do, think like we do, act like we do. Each of us is unique, and our aloneness is the other side of our uniqueness. The question is whether we let our aloneness become loneliness or whether we allow it to lead us into solitude. Loneliness is painful; solitude is peaceful. Loneliness makes us cling to others in desperation; solitude allows us to respect others in their uniqueness and create community. Letting our aloneness grow into solitude and not into loneliness is a lifelong struggle. It requires conscious choices about whom to be with, what to study, how to pray, and when to ask for counsel. But wise choices will help us to find the solitude where our hearts can grow in love (January 18)" (36:226).

Solitude as a Place for Prayer

It is not surprising that we have arrived at this point. Later we will move on to the third main concept in Nouwen's spirituality, prayer. For where else, other than in solitude, can we find a place where our prayer is most intense. In prayer the whole of human existence resounds, in all its joy and sorrow. In prayer we are asked "to give up all that divides us from others so that we can *become* those we pray for and let God touch them in us" (11:32).

Solitude, Community, and Ministry

Nouwen's books reveal that he himself also suffered deeply from loneliness and continued to do so to the very end of his life. For example, there was the loneliness that was part and parcel of his conscious choice to become a priest, his life that ran such a different course from the other people in his family. He did not hesitate to issue personal accounts of this loneliness. The propensity to run away from it, to flee from it, was a fact that he recognized very well and illustrates through the example of his own life. The realization that he was gradually becoming a well-known personality in the United States could easily have tempted him to flee into fame and prestige. Yet he also learned that you get nowhere with these often unconscious flights; on the contrary, they lead you further and further from home so that you're deeper in the doldrums than you were before.

That's why Nouwen always sought out people who would bring him back to the painful place of solitude — for example, John Eudes in the monastery and Père Thomas at Trosly. "Spiritual direction" is not an explicit theme in Nouwen's work, but it was something to which he continually submitted in order to gain insight into his own spiritual process.[40] We see that gradually the community as a whole, particularly at Daybreak, took over this guiding role. In pastoral consultations at Daybreak there was a mutuality of support and correction in which the sensitive antennae of the handicapped people served as signals.

As pastor, Nouwen provided leadership in this process, but he also took part in it himself. It seemed as if his own loneliness had been changed for the good with his arrival at L'Arche, that a fruitful balance had developed between the two poles, loneliness and solitude.[41] In any case his first books and those from his Yale years deal more with loneliness than the more recent ones do. This had to do with a deeper understanding of his own vocation to agree to be a "father," to be present for the countless lonely, scattered sons and daughters, so visible in the handicapped people of L'Arche. Now I can understand why Nouwen worked so hard during his last years for a new prayer center at Daybreak, for "prayer is the breath of the Christian community" (11:30–31). The prospectus for the future retreat center states, "Daybreak's strength comes from its spiritual foundation, and communal worship is an important part of life here. The new Daysprings chapel will enable the community and its friends to stay in touch with the spiritual dimension of daily living, thereby deepening their faith and vocation."[42]

– 12 –

PRAYER

Plumbing the Depths

People are *called*, and when they follow the gentle urging of the voice that calls them they are led, despite everything to the contrary, to a place of "green pastures." These are the grassy plains that, step by step, they have recovered from their own barren *loneliness*. It's a journey through a wasted and empty landscape, and every stop along the way is only temporary. The true and final dwelling place is yet to come and is never within their reach. From the mountaintops of our lives we must go back down into the valleys, to the tedious daily grind, to the boring long haul, to the blaring newspaper headlines that announce death and destruction. But the rough journey has taught us something. We've brought something with us, an outlook, a vision. An encounter has taken place. We've made a discovery beneath the surface of the gray drudgery of ordinary existence. We've discovered that a conversation is possible, that our cry from the depths has found a willing listener, that our far-reaching, exhausted words come back to us filled.

Nouwen discusses this conversation in a variety of ways. Prayer (for that's what this inner conversation is called) forms the very pulse of his work. In the midst of everything that he was engaged in, prayer was his constant plumb line. If anything goes wrong with prayer, then everything else is up in the air. "Prayer makes men contemplative and attentive. In place of manipulating, the man who prays stands receptive before the world. He no longer grabs but caresses, he no longer bites but kisses, he no longer examines but admires" (2:24).

The Pulse of the World (With Open Hands)

One of Nouwen's first books dealt explicitly with prayer, *With Open Hands* (3). In conjunction with this third key concept, "prayer," I want to examine that book more deeply. I would call *With Open Hands* the basis for Nouwen's further work. It was written as a pamphlet, a program. Here the writer makes his appearance, the man who would repeat this basic concept in many other books, expanding, deepening, and modifying it. There's no sign of the tone that ran through Nouwen's first book, *Intimacy* (1969). This is no scholarly, pedantic professor, but a human being involved with others and with their inner lives. The book's writing style searches for simplicity and rest. The choice of language corresponds with what it hopes to describe. Abstraction is avoided as much as possible; examples out of everyday life must support the whole of the language. An evocative power is noticeable in the language for the first time.

The writer has begun to find his "place." Throughout the book the same message resounds: this is what we should be concerned about for the future of the church and the faith; all the rest may be important (religious themes, etc.), but they easily serve as so much dead weight in the human journey toward truth and God, toward wholeness and justice. From the start Nouwen felt that although talking and writing about prayer may be theologically interesting, it doesn't really help beyond that — at least it wasn't helpful to him. Rather than speaking about prayer, he and his students and fellow teachers began to put together a concrete collection of prayers. Their goal was not to produce a beautiful literary product, but by means of these words, written in deep tranquility, to gain access to their own hearts — places where God may not have been allowed to enter, places often haunted by the past and uncertain of the future. Only then would they talk about prayer and try to express it in words, sharing their experiences.

This was how the book was written. *With Open Hands* deals with the interior movement of the heart. In short, accessible chapters we become acquainted with ourselves — no matter how cramped our lives may be, no matter how tightly clenched our fists (3:12), no matter how devoid we are of exterior and interior silence, no matter how preoccupied we are with getting and having things in order to make ourselves invulnerable. Thus hope is strangled within us, rendering us dead even as we live. "Only if you pray with hope can you break through the barriers of death" (3:84). This is the birth of compassion. "For in prayer, you not only profess that man is man and God is God, but also, that your neighbor is your fellowman, that is, a man alongside you" (3:102).

Here is the beginning of a radical commitment to the other. In this sense prayer is even revolutionary. "Praying means breaking through the veil of existence and allowing yourself to be led by the vision which has become real to you" (33:142). Prayer makes people free, spectacularly free. Prayer makes people vulnerable because it was into open hands that nails were driven. People who pray are the heralds of a new world; they see prayer as the pulse of the world in which we live.

God Breathes in Us (from Illusion to Prayer)

Nouwen also wrote extensively about prayer in his book *Reaching Out* (8). You notice that during his first years at Yale he was intensively occupied with prayer, both in his research and in his personal life. We already said that *Reaching Out* could be described as the high point of his authorship during the Yale period, when he became very personal for the first time and let his own experience play a role. In comparison with *With Open Hands*, the ground here is ploughed even more deeply. More theology comes into view and the human person, in his or her inability to pray, is taken more seriously. The environment of the monastery at Genesee, where he wrote the last chapter of *Reaching Out*, did the work of purification.

Henri explained how a sort of illusion of immortality stands in the way of our longing to pray because "we keep giving an eternal value to the things we own, the people we know, the plans we have, and the successes we 'collect' " (8:82).

This illusion of immortality has two sides, sentimentality and violence, and is visible in a tyrant such as Hitler, who murdered millions of people and at the same time was brought to tears when he took a little girl on his lap. It is "a symptom of the illusion that our lives belong to us" (8:84). These illusions pursue us even in our dreams, so deep are they within us. However, "when we move from illusion to prayer, we move from the human shelter to the house of God" (8:86). The pages that follow are among the most impressive that I have read from Nouwen. The most basic human question, namely, the attainability of God, is addressed here, questions that go beyond evidence and beyond any possible defense. And at this point Nouwen tunnels through and runs into a paradox, the main paradox of prayer. "The paradox of prayer is that we have to learn how to pray while we can only receive it as a gift" (8:87). "We cannot force God into a relationship. God comes to us on his own initiative, and no discipline, effort, or ascetic practice can make him come. All mystics stress with an impressive unanimity that prayer is 'grace,' that is, a free gift from God, to which we can only respond with gratitude. But they hasten to add that this precious gift indeed is within our reach" (8:88). Nouwen continues putting it differently in order to help his readers, to lead them into the free space where the human being really lives and God is almost present. "Prayer, therefore, is God's breathing in us, by which we become part of the intimacy of God's inner life, and by which we are born anew" (8:89).

Can Prayer Be Learned?

Those who delve into the literature about prayer discover that there are different prayer traditions. Eastern Orthodoxy has developed a particularly rich spirituality of prayer down through the centuries, both in its monasteries and in its parish life. There

are different schools of prayer, but the school known as hesy-
chasm comes especially to mind. The Jesus Prayer was developed
within this hesychastic tradition, a "technique" used to live according to the quotation from St. Paul in which he says that we
must pray unceasingly. "Pray at all times, pray without ceasing,
thankful for all, because that is the will of God in Christ Jesus
for you" (1 Thess. 5:16–18). Nouwen gave numerous classes on
these different traditions, sounding out, as it were, their useful-
ness for people today as a sort of "tool" (8). For despite the
paradox of prayer described above, it is possible to learn to pray.
Many people before us, and certainly many among us, are willing
to share their prayer life. You don't always have to begin from
absolute zero.

Equally helpful are those places where you can experience the
continuous prayer that has been going on there for centuries:
monasteries, chapels, and churches. In those places you seem to
walk right into prayer. This discipline has been especially neglected
in pastoral training programs. It's not for nothing that Nouwen
emphasized prayer so frequently in his books about ministry.
To extensively explore the traditions of the "Jesus Prayer," "the
prayer of the heart," or "interior prayer" in this book would take
us too far off the track, but we can still demonstrate what Nouwen did with them. He called them "a murmuring stream that
continues underneath the many waves of every day and opens
the possibility of living in the world without being of it and of
reaching out to our God from the center of our solitude" (8:105).

Pray without Ceasing

Nouwen gave an even clearer sketch of "prayer without ceasing" in the chapter "Prayer and Thought," which is included in
Clowning in Rome (11). How can this prayer without ceasing
be achieved in our age? We can no longer emulate the way the
Russian pilgrim practiced the Jesus Prayer in his familiar book,
no matter how commendable his efforts.[43] The starting point for
Nouwen is that prayer is not something extra that you fit in with

everything else. We must pray not "as a part of life, but as all of life" (11:61). Prayer must be so much a part of us that it becomes like breathing; "praying is like breathing" (11:61). How is this done? Or rather, "How can thinking become praying?" (11:63).

We just can't get around the fact that we're always thinking, that there's always a stream of thought passing through us. There is no moment when we're not thinking, both active "reflective thinking" and passive "prereflective thinking" (11:66). We cannot think about nothing, not even in our sleep. "Our thought processes reach even deeper than our reflective moments and our uncontrolled mental wanderings" (11:67). This stream of thought can be a burden, but it can also be a gift, "the cradle where sorrow (disturbing graffiti) and joy (gratitude) are born" (11:69). That's why "This unceasing thinking that lies at the core of our humanity needs to be converted slowly but persistently into unceasing prayer" (11:69).

Unceasing prayer is not something like continuously thinking about God. It is something else. Nouwen is quite precise and gives more or less a "definition" of prayer: "To pray, I think, does not mean to think about God in contrast to thinking about other things, or to spend time with God instead of spending time with other people. Rather, it means to think and live in the presence of God" (11:70). Every moment must find its origin in this prayer and must therefore not be isolated from our daily preoccupations. This requires a "converting...from a self-centered monologue to a God-centered dialogue" (11:70–71). It is a learning process in which we can "lead all our thoughts out of their fearful isolation into a fearless conversation with God" (11:71).

Prayer is something very different from introspection, which is too psychological. Introspection is necessary, but it is only partial. "Introspection can cause paralyzing worries or unproductive self-gratification" (11:72). In prayer we are actually led away from this inner self. Indeed, "Prayer is the joyful affirmation that God knows our minds and hearts" (11:72).

This reversal is difficult because we are not inclined to put everything before God, but to keep our business outside the dialogue. This is "the road to idolatry." So because we withhold things from the Eternal, because we refuse to honor God and give God priority, "unceasing prayer is a continuous battle against idolatry." But then how can we make a start at this "loving conversation with God"?

This can happen by means of good discipline. "Discipline means that something very specific and concrete needs to be done to create the context in which a life of uninterrupted prayer can develop. Unceasing prayer requires the discipline of prayer exercises" (11:76). This is the discipline of contemplative prayer, "in which we attentively look at God" (11:77). We can "see" God through Jesus himself (11:78). "Contemplative prayer can be described as an imagining of Christ, letting him enter fully into our consciousness so that he becomes the icon always present in our inner room" (11:78).

After saying this, Nouwen is eager to get down to practical matters. For example, he suggests that every night before going to sleep we meditate on the Bible passage from the following day's reading. By doing this, the text goes with us through the night and stays with us. We can also meditate on the text during the next day for an hour or so. The result is that the text starts to read us. A certain familiarity and continuity in companionship with God begins to grow. God starts to speak in us, Jesus becomes "a beautiful icon" during this "empty time."[44]

Prayer and Social Involvement

Obviously, prayer has a tremendous influence on everything we do. From his very first book, Nouwen emphasized that prayer has everything to do with all of life's activities. According to him, prayer is wrongly associated with a pious and devotional attitude and nothing more. Prayer then deteriorates into an individual line of communication upward where the pious soul is strengthened apart from its social environment. The result of this view of prayer is a disengaged "I" in relationship with an isolated God, a view still widely held by many. That's why prayer should "never become the most individualistic expression of the most individualistic emotion, but should always remain embedded in the life of the community of which we are part" (8:109). Not that there is anything wrong with refreshing the individual soul, but if prayer remains there, a sort of half-spirituality develops.

It was in the spirit of the late 1960s that Nouwen spoke about prayer and revolution in *With Open Hands*. I have not encountered such strong radical social criticism in any of his following books, although he did continue to emphasize the relationship between prayer and action. Prayer is "the first expression of human solidarity," wrote Nouwen in his most scholarly book, *Compassion: A Reflection on the Christian Life*. It is "the very beat of a compassionate heart" (16:109). "To pray for others means to make them part of ourselves" (16:110). Nouwen took great care to keep prayer and action together. "Prayer without action grows into powerless pietism, and action without prayer degenerates into questionable manipulation" (16:116–17). The possibility that these polarities might become separated came to life before his very eyes during his time in Latin America. In *Gracias* (18) we repeatedly read that without prayer, active people become hard and embittered as the desired results elude them. Indeed, it was on this point that Nouwen criticized particular tendencies within liberation theology, as we have seen, and he confronted Gutiérrez with them, whose strength was precisely in radically holding together prayer and active involvement.

In Nouwen's report of the very dangerous situation in Guatemala at that time, where people had their backs against the wall and were able to remain hopeful against all better judgment, that is where prayer "occurs" in its full dimensions and glory. "When malnutrition, poor health, poor housing, low pay, and long, tiring work mark life every day; when terror fills the air and torture and death are a constant threat, the human heart has to choose between despair and hope, between resignation to the power of darkness or a defiant reaching out to the light, between victimization and liberation. It is an inner choice, not dependent on outer conditions but on the will to claim one's freedom whatever the circumstances. To cry out to the God of life in the midst of darkness, to hold on to joy while walking in a valley of tears, to keep speaking of peace when sounds of war fill the air — that is what prayer is about" (19:103).

If I see it correctly, at the point of "prayer and involvement" there was a shift in Nouwen's vision of prayer. He began in *With Open Hands* with a stance that was radically critical of society, and in his books just before and during the Latin American experience he became more involved in society. In Western Europe, someone is called a political radical if he or she envisions a different way of organizing society and is severely and actively critical of the capitalistic system. Social involvement is a more moderate approach. After Latin America it seems to me that Nouwen's emphasis on social involvement also began declining, as becomes evident in the chapter on prayer in one of his last books, *Here and Now* (33). Social resistance and political involvement are indeed present, but are less concrete and more universal. This is easy to understand, because it makes a difference whether you live among people who are economically and materially poor, as in Latin America, or live in a community of mentally handicapped. The spirit of the times is still making its influence felt. Social and political involvement are not so "in" as we approach the end of the millennium. The question thus remains whether Nouwen himself succeeded in holding together the unity of prayer and involvement that he advocated.

Nouwen's Own Struggle with Prayer

As we have said, there is a big difference between writing about prayer and trying to make prayer an integral component of your life. Nouwen would be the first to acknowledge this. The tension in his work is always palpable, and his conclusion is that writing about the spiritual life acquires real depth only if it also relates to the individual's very personal struggle. Nouwen's writing also reveals periods of spiritually barren valleys, aridity, and the inability to pray. These alternate with moments of intensive involvement and joy. And usually they are woven together in an uncontrollable intensity. "There are many times when I cannot pray, when I am too tired to read the Gospels, too restless to have spiritual thoughts, too depressed to find words for God, or too exhausted to do anything" (21:11). But he knows that he must keep going, that even in times of dryness God blesses us with the promise of rain. Prayer and discipline belong together; no single disciple can do without them. "In the Christian life, discipline is the human effort to unveil what has been covered, to bring to the foreground what has remained hidden, and to put on the lampstand what has been kept under a basket. It is like raking away the leaves that cover the pathways in the garden of our soul. Discipline enables the revelation of God's divine Spirit in us" (16:90).

Then there is the space of silence in which prayer can thrive. When everything around us and within us is quiet, when the interior and exterior voices are calmed, then the possibility of achieving harmony arises, of being able to hear the voice of the One. During his seven months in the monastery, Nouwen learned how purifying silence can be. One day when he had to leave the monastery for the city, he came back and wrote, "With the diminishing of silence, I had ever more sharply the feeling that I was being interiorly contaminated" (9:113).[45]

We will likely spend our whole lives searching for the balance between exterior and interior, between the longing of a tormented soul and the fierce attraction of a vital but contaminated life. Perhaps the balance that we seek here is best reached when we abandon our desperate desire for it. To want to attain something in the realm of the spiritual life can easily turn into a kind of spasm. But spirituality is bypassing this insistence that something happen and arriving in the realm of trust. If we are faithful to the present moment and to our prayers, God does the rest. In the hectic, noisy world of the "barrio" in the giant city of Lima, Nouwen wrote: "Yet without this one-hour-a-day for God, my life loses its coherency and I start experiencing my days as a series of random incidents and accidents. My hour in the Carmelite chapel is more important than I can fully know myself. It is not an hour of deep prayer, nor a time in which I experience a special closeness to God; it is not a period of serious attentiveness to the divine mysteries. I wish it were! On the contrary, it is full of distractions, inner restlessness, sleepiness, confusion, and boredom. It seldom, if ever, pleases my senses. But the simple fact of being for one hour in the presence of the Lord and of showing him all that I feel, think, sense, and experience, without trying to hide anything, must please him. Somehow, somewhere, I know that he loves me, even though I do not feel that love as I can feel a human embrace, even though I do not hear a voice as I hear human words of consolation, even though I do not see a smile as I can see a human face. Still the Lord speaks to me, looks at me, and embraces me there, where I am still unable to notice it" (18:69).

Is it this faithful, watchful attitude of a searching person that brings results? For many, and I am among them, that's a good question. Can we expect a response, does the sunlight break through the rainy heavens every now and then? Will God ever show himself, even if only for a moment? If we look concretely at Nouwen's life, do we see any progress, was there any development in his spiritual life, were his efforts ever rewarded? Did prayer, discipline, and silence bring him to an encounter? In short, can the mystical experience, the mystic's "seeing, if only for a moment," be traced in Nouwen's life and work? Or are these questions of an impatient soul, a spiritual utilitarian (indeed, now look who's talking about results!).

Nouwen lifted up the edge of the veil in 1988 when he wrote a new foreword for one of his first books, *With Open Hands*. "Up to now I have been spared bitterness. The spiritual battle to open my hands and to keep them open has led me constantly deeper inside, into the mysteries of God's boundless love and has caused me to realize more and more that prayer is above all a gift to be received with gratitude. One thing is certain. My longing to pray is increasing steadily, so strongly that it has become more and more desirable for me to be alone with God, even when I have nothing to say or to ask for. In the quiet hours I experience what I have written about in this book: silence, acceptance, hope, compassion, and prophetic criticism, and I discover that I can attain the whole world in the heart of God" (3).

"Led constantly deeper inside" were the few words that Nouwen devoted to any spiritual progress he may have undergone. Indeed, questions regarding results in the spiritual life are foolhardy questions. God cannot be forced, even though we may do our best. Certainly there are the blessed few among us who see even further, to whom it has been given to see more. In none of his writings have I detected that Nouwen is a mystic in this sense, let alone that he called himself one.[46] Rather he is a spy in the promised land who renders an account of his own spiritual harvest, including in the form of a prayer.[47] "So I am praying while not knowing how to pray. I am resting while feeling restless, at peace while tempted, safe while still anxious, surrounded by a cloud of light while still in darkness, in love while still doubting" (23:134).

The Paradox of Prayer (the Ever-Present Absence)

All that has been said up to now about prayer may give the impression that prayer is just a matter of pure human effort, something that emanates from us to God, something that we do with ease or with difficulty, so that we either give up or get to work. The fact that God also plays a role, and a very active one at that, disappears from the picture. Here we also bump into something that we mentioned earlier: the paradox of prayer, a paradox that is expressed both theologically as well as within the context of people's experience whenever the discussion turns to the absence and presence of God. Now we seem to be heavily involved in theology, but it is striking how down to earth Nouwen brought this "heavy" theme. "Here we touch the heart of prayer since here it becomes manifest that in prayer the distinction between God's presence and God's absence no longer really distinguishes. In prayer, God's presence is never separated from his absence and God's absence is never separated from his presence. His presence is so much beyond the human experience of being together that it quite easily is perceived as absence" (8:90). And in concluding this train of thought he says, "It is in the center of our longing for the absent God that we discover his footprints, and realize that our desire to love God is born out of the love with which he has touched us" (8:91). This brings us to the fourth key concept of Nouwen's spirituality: God's first love.

– 13 –

THE FIRST LOVE

"O Lord, look with favor on us, your people, and impart your love to us — not as an idea or concept, but as a lived experience. We can only love each other because you have loved us first. Let us know that first love so that we can see all human love as a reflection of a greater love, a love without conditions and limitations" (15:52).

The supporting power of God's love is present and reverberates in all human activity. No, not at first sight, nor at first sound, but in hidden ways this love sings a song in every human heart and plays a role in the history of the world. This love is inescapable and steadfast, never demanding but inviting. It is a driving force that can be confessed in faith and experienced in prayer. Proper prayer brings us to the place of that first love. If we open our eyes, everything is bathed in its strong light; if we separate our folded hands, they are ready to work out of this Light on the darkness in this world. "We have love because He has first loved us" (1 John 4:19). That is the way the kingdom of God is ordered.

We saw that our *vocation* is grounded in the One who calls, our *solitude* is continually forged into a gift from a higher power, our *prayer* is not an endless cry to a blank wall because God leads us in prayer. And now we are at the place where all this comes from: the first love, the Eternal One.

Because God First Loved Us

The theme of the first love is already present in Nouwen's first book, the heart of which lies in the above-mentioned text from the first letter of John. In *Intimacy* he discusses the subject in conversation with psychology (Freud especially), which says that these lofty sentiments are mere projections, that "religion is the continuation of infantile life and that God is the projection of the ever-present desire for shelter" (1:10). Following the German psychiatrist Binswanger, Nouwen turns Freud around: "God is not the prolongation of the child's relationship with his dad, but the child's feeling for his dad is a concretizing of an idea born of his most fundamental relation to his Creator. In other words, we couldn't love our father if God had not loved us first. *But here we have left the field of psychology*" (11:11; italics mine). And a little further on Nouwen summarizes: "Our religious sentiment will never be mature (1) if God is not the Other, (2) if prayer is not a dialogue, and (3) if religion is not a source of creative autonomy" (1:11–12).

It is striking how faithful Nouwen remained over the years to the theological opinions expressed in this early work. He felt intuitively that the whole broad field of psychology asked questions only "from below," but very pointed and necessary ones. As a psychologist he was thoroughly conscious of this, but these questions revealed only one side of the coin, ensnaring and stifling any vision of this first love. Even so, we must be well aware that this first love is never something separate, pure, and at our disposal. It is intertwined in all the other love stories of humankind. Whenever this fact is overlooked, the activity of love seizes up; it gets overheated as it were because it has no outlet, no final place where it is being collected. For this reason Nouwen distinguishes this activity of love and speaks about a first and a second love. "The love that often leaves us doubtful, frustrated, angry, and resentful is the second love, that is to say, the affirmation, affection, sympathy, encouragement, and support that we receive from our parents, teachers, spouses, and friends. We all know how limited, broken, and very fragile that love is. Behind the many expressions of this second love there is always the chance of rejection, withdrawal, punishment, blackmail, violence, and even hatred.... Often it seems that beneath the pleasantries of daily life there are many gaping wounds that carry such names as: abandonment, betrayal, rejection, rupture, and loss. These are all the shadow side of the second love and reveal the darkness that never completely leaves the human heart" (25:25–26).

Elsewhere he expands upon this and speaks about three types of love. The third love is the outermost circle. It is the love in the broader sense, among human groups and peoples. The second love, which we already have seen, is the love of those nearest to us, the inner circle, family, friends, colleagues, relatives. "I dare now to say that all relationships in life, love relationships, friendships, community relationships, yes even relationships among people on a national or international level, find their source and ultimately their meaning in the first love of God." And Nouwen typifies the theological concept of "world" as "the human love that has become separated from God's first love."[48] This is an extremely radical insight because the efforts made on behalf of the world can become unconditional in this way. "Whenever you have come to know the first love in your heart, the whole world can belong to you without your expecting what it cannot give."[49]

You Are My Beloved

A voice calls out from this first love. The loving activity between God and humankind is not a static situation. Distinctions such as first, second, and third love can come across as too systematic. Even though the relationship is characterized by dynamism and motion, there is also urgency and impatience. Love wants her first love to be reciprocated; it pines like one who is without love. Nouwen emphasizes this dynamic (emanating from God and then moving on from us) in a very penetrating way in his book *Life of the Beloved* (28). His starting point is the text "You are my Son, the beloved; in you I am well satisfied" (Mark 1:11). "We are intimately loved long before our parents, teachers, spouses, children and friends loved or wounded us. That's the truth of our lives. That's the truth I want you to claim for yourself. That's the truth spoken by the voice that says, 'You are my Beloved.' Listening to that voice with great inner attentiveness, I hear at my center words that say: 'I have called you by name, from the very beginning. You are mine and I am yours. You are my Beloved, on you my favor rests. I have molded you in the depths of the earth and knitted you together in your mother's womb. I have carved you in the palms of my hands and hidden you in the shadow of my embrace. I look at you with infinite tenderness and care for you with a care more intimate than that of a mother for her child. I have counted every hair on your head and guided you at every step. Wherever you go, I go with you, and wherever you rest, I keep watch. I will give you food that will satisfy all your hunger and drink that will quench all your thirst. I will not hide my face from you. You know me as your own as I know you as my own. You belong to me. I am your father, your mother, your brother, your sister, your lover and your spouse . . . yes, even your child . . . wherever you are I will be. Nothing will ever separate us. We are one' " (28:30–31).

There's something extraordinarily positive about this book. You see that Nouwen must have felt at home at Daybreak, that he experienced the three types of love being manifest there, that the first love was and had to be everything, especially in those vulnerable surroundings, otherwise the whole community would falter. More than that, for Henri the severely handicapped Adam became "the preferable mediator of the first love" (34/4:25).

Looking at the whole picture, it is remarkable that in all of Nouwen's works, where the first love is such a central concept, there is no mention of a very particular Bible verse which also deals with the first love. I refer to the text from Revelation 2:4 (certainly not unfamiliar) which says that the community at Ephesus has forsaken its first love: "But I say to you that you have forsaken your first love."[50] This strong ethical appeal from the prophet of Patmos, this critical admonition that people had not accepted the invitation to love, with all its social consequences, is something that Nouwen seems to have disregarded when he speaks and writes so positively, so affirmatively. It is as if he had a problem giving shape to this prophetic outburst or integrating it into his arguments, since he was probably afraid of tarnishing the priestly speech that he used to express himself.[51]

Wet Ground in the Desert

As always, Nouwen's own life was the sounding board for testing and tasting this first love,[52] for feeling living water on his lips amid the dryness of daily existence. At Genesee he wrote in his diary how difficult it was for him to give and to receive love. There, in the monastery, in that place for reflection, this revelation came to light. Indeed, the monks there did not gaze into his eyes; they did not idolize him. For them he was only a fellow brother. The adulation that he had experienced so regularly as a renowned writer in many of the places he had visited was non-existent here. This was very recognizable when he wrote, "My idea of love proves to be exclusive: 'You only love me truly if you love others less'; possessive: 'If you really love me, I want you to pay special attention to me'; and manipulative: 'When you love me, you will do extra things for me.' Well, this idea of love easily leads to vanity: 'You must see something very special in me'; to jealousy: 'Why are you now suddenly so interested in someone else and not in me?' and to anger: 'I am going to let you know that you have let me down and rejected me'" (9:67).

For Nouwen the monastery was a place of purification where he came to the discovery that the highly prized "love of neighbor" is often no more than "a tentative, partial, or momentary attraction" (9:67). From the monks Nouwen learned, often against his will, that God is entitled to the first place, that all others find their existence in this giving love. It is certainly possible that a fellow human being will remind me of the first place to which God is entitled, and in so doing that person will become a means, a vehicle, but that means can never become the final goal of love. "It is exactly in the preciousness of the individual person that the eternal love of God is refracted and becomes the basis of a community of love" (9:68). To dig up this treasure by yourself and with others is the purpose of the spiritual way. "The first is: Hear, Israel, the Lord our God, is Lord Alone, and you shall love the Lord, your God, with your whole heart and your whole soul and your whole mind and your whole strength. The second is this: You shall love your neighbor as yourself" (Mark 12:30, 31). "The second is...." There is a unity and diversity in the relationship — covenant — between God and neighbor. The second commandment is certainly like the first, but still remains the second commandment and not the first.[53]

So there is not and cannot be any rivalry between the first and second loves, between the first and second commandments. There is certainly a sequence and rank, not to put people in second place, but to protect them against themselves and to incorporate them into the immense space of love. Then, step by step, a fruitful life matures.[54] "Every time you listen with great attentiveness to the voice that calls you the Beloved, you will discover within yourself a desire to hear that voice longer and more deeply. It is like discovering a well in the desert. Once you have touched wet ground, you want to dig deeper. I have been doing a lot of digging lately and I know that I am just beginning to see a little stream bubbling up through the dry sand. I have to keep digging because that little stream comes from a huge reservoir beneath the desert of my life" (28:31).

– 14 –

BEYOND DEATH

Our whole world is in the grip of death, at least it seems that way. With fierce eagerness, death clamps its bold tentacles around us — and just hauls us in! Its harvest appears many times greater than the fruit of love, and the result is a virtual battlefield: hunger, war, violence, a path of destruction in the environment. Death is the order of the day. Who can deny it? Just look around you. And look at people's personal lives; isn't there always some degree of sorrow? The deterioration of the elderly, persistent sicknesses that ravage the lives of so many people. Look at yourself. It can happen just like that. Like a thief in the night death sneaks in and finds you. Anxiety grips your heart. Is this what life is about? Is life no more than one big hopeless black hole? When everything ends in death, what's the point of this first, second, third love! I could go on forever with this long litany of questions, with these lonely reflections of the frightened human heart. A thousand variations of these cries of the heart rumble through everyone's head; they strike like long and heavy waves, like foaming surf pounding against the shore. Is there no choice but to drown in these questions? Are we doomed to be pulled under in the pain of death and destruction? Is there Someone who can help? Is there intimacy, a hand on your shoulder, a companion who will accompany you? Is there perhaps the seed of an answer that will push my questions in another direction so that I can breathe again?

Wrestling with death and the attempt to search for a hesitant answer-in-faith are profoundly present in Nouwen's books. These

110

are no abstract reflections. "Death" as a problem area waiting to be investigated did not interest him. His concern was with concrete people in his own environment who were confronted with death and who then became the object of his reflections: his mother, his sister-in-law Marina, Père Thomas at Trosly, his secretary Connie Ellis at Daybreak, and the many victims of AIDS among his friends.[55] He called on these people and helped them, as he did when he visited the dying Cardinal Bernardin of Chicago. "This conversation was a great help to me," said Bernardin. "It removed some of my anxiety or fear about death for myself."[56] Nouwen wanted to give inevitable death a religious place in his life. He did not want to shut death out but to incorporate it fully into his own spirituality. When an end comes to someone's human life, how can we deal with it "in faith"? Not only later, when death actually appears, but even now!

"We hesitantly come forth out of the darkness of birth and slowly vanish into the darkness of death. We move from dust to dust, from unknown to unknown, from mystery to mystery. We try to keep a vital balance on the thin rope that is stretched between two definitive endings we have never seen or understood. We are surrounded by the reality of the unseen, which fills every part of our life with a moment of terror but at the same time holds the secret mystery of our being alive" (4:90–91).

Aging and Death

"Even to your old age I am the same, even when your hair is gray I will bear you; It is I who have done this, I who will continue, and I who will carry you to safety" (Isa. 46:4).

A concern for these pressing questions is part of the human *vocation*. In the *solitude* of the individual heart death is always lurking. There, in that solitude, is where the struggle takes place, a struggle between light and darkness in which *prayer* (sometimes) offers a way out, because the agonizing questions have been taken up by the All-Embracing and come to rest in the *first love* of the Eternal.

In *Aging*, a book about old age, we see the first evidence of
Nouwen's reflection on death. In the journey through life, the way
to old age can go in either of two directions. A person can experience growing old as a way to darkness or as a way to light. All
around us, the first way receives the most attention and study.
Nouwen speaks out for the elderly and warns society that whenever people no longer honor the elderly as prophets (6:16), they
cut themselves off from a vital life experience and in so doing
threaten society with disintegration. This cutting off has direct
consequences for the elderly themselves; they become completely
isolated. "If segregation is rejection by society, desolation is often
experienced as a 'rejection' by one's friends" (6:32). But the most
destructive consequence is ultimately the loss of one's self. "He
who has lost his most inner self has nothing left to live for"
(6:37). We know that is true with many elderly people who are
living entirely in the past. "I am who I was" (6:40). "They have
opened the innermost room of their sanctuary and allowed the
evil forces to take possession of it" (6:40).

But there is also another path: the path toward the light. This
path takes shape in mid-life (6:67). It is the path from a life
full of wishes to a life full of hope. Wishes are linked to "concrete objects" (6:64). "Hope is open-ended, built on the trust that
the other will fulfill his or her promises" (6:64). Hope generates
humor, which is indispensable in aging. "Humor is knowledge
with a soft smile" (6:71). Thus the insight is awakened that produces an integrated life "in which the distinction between life and
death slowly loses its pain" (6:75).[57]

Old age is also a fascinating feature in the paintings of Rembrandt. In the faces that he painted you can see how light and
darkness are mixed in a person's life, and you can also see
whether the victor in the struggle was embitterment or fulfilled
hope. "Some of Rembrandt's most stunning portraits are of old
people, and his most gripping self-portraits are made during his
last years.... As Rembrandt's own life moves toward the shadows of old age, as his success wanes, and the exterior splendor
of his life diminishes, he comes more in touch with the immense
beauty of the interior life" (29:88–99).

Detachment from "the World"

"Detachment" is the spiritual insight that Nouwen wanted to impress upon his readers. You do not have to hold on for dear life to the things around you, the people around you, or the world around you, and finally you don't even have to hold on to yourself. In the monastery he sighed, "I am ever more convinced that I have not yet left the world" (9). This conclusion did not lead Nouwen to renounce anything or to abandon the world. On the contrary, only the one who remains detached in the world is free and able to act in freedom. This is also the heart of his ethics, as we will later see. The biblical instruction to be in the world but not of the world comes up regularly in his books. In this detachment from the world lies the human spiritual pilgrimage and the beginnings of an answer to the great questions about death.

Those who make this biblically centered pilgrimage and are led through it by qualified fellow pilgrims must come to terms with their own origins, the point at which God once joined us. Those who rediscover these origins also come to know that the first love does not end at the biological borders of death. When we learn to die in this way our life begins to bear fruit, both for ourselves and especially for those who come after us. In our dying we teach them about living. In his beautiful book about Guatemala, Nouwen describes how the life of the murdered priest Stan gave life to his successor John. "Stan's death was John's life" (19:21). This is how the life of Jesus must be seen: that his dying became life-giving for his disciples. "Without the death and resurrection of Jesus the Gospel is a beautiful tale about an exceptionally saintly person, a tale that might inspire good thoughts and great deeds; but there are other stories of that sort. The Gospel is, first and foremost, the story of the death and resurrection of Jesus, and that story constitutes the core of the spiritual life" (22:27).

The Greatest Gift

This fruitfulness that overcomes death seems to me Henri's real contribution to the spiritual concern about death. The many lines of thought that appear in several of his books come together in *Our Greatest Gift* (31). In this book he tightens up all the insights made so far. "Can we wait for our death as for a friend who wants to welcome us home?" (31:xiii). The task that he gives himself is this: "I wanted to write about befriending my death so that it can become my best gift to the world I love so much" (31:xvii). "When I myself am able to befriend death, I will be able to help others do the same. That is the work of this little book" (31:6).

This is typical of Nouwen: the best way to really learn what it is you're talking about is to experience it yourself. In this case: those who have never looked their own death in the face cannot possibly assist someone who is dying. People die, and there are people who want to assist the dying. Therefore *Our Greatest Gift* (31) contains two parts, one about "a good death" and another about "good care." The one leads into the other. The important question is: from a spiritual perspective, what does it mean to look your own death in the face?

First of all, it means that we realize that we are children of God, that we undergo a "second childhood" and learn to be dependent again (31:14). This is in direct opposition to our achievement-based culture. "Once we have come to the deep inner knowledge — a knowledge more of the heart than of the mind — that we are born out of love and will die into love, that every part of our being is deeply rooted in love and that this love is our true Father and Mother, then all forms of evil, illness, and death lose their final power over us" (31:17).

Second, it means that we learn to appreciate that as human beings we are all sisters and brothers. Nouwen raises the banal statement "we're all going to die anyway" to a higher plane. "I am convinced that it is this joy — the joy of being the same as others, of belonging to one human family — that allows us to die well" (31:26). Death bonds us in a "great human sameness"

(31:28). "We all die poor" (31:31). And this solidarity is a source of hope for those who die unjustly (31:32).

Third, it means that once we have died, we become parents for future generations. As Jesus himself said in John 16:7, it is good for his disciples that he goes away. Not only the death of Jesus, but also our own death can become fruitful for others. "Here is the most hope-giving aspect of death. Our death may be the end of our success, our productivity, our fame, or our importance among people, but it is not the end of our fruitfulness" (31:38). "So my death will indeed be a rebirth. Something new will come to be, something about which I cannot say or think much. It lies beyond my own chronology. It is something that will last and carry on from generation to generation. In this way, I become a new parent, a parent of the future" (31:42–43).

The second part about "good care" is a counterpart to the first part of the book.[58] I will treat the concept of caring with other typical Nouwen concepts in the next part of this book, the section on ethics.

A Glimpse of the Other Side

"Am I afraid to die? I am every time I let myself be seduced by the noisy voices of my world telling me that my 'little self' is all I have and advising me to cling to it with all my might. But when I let these voices move to the background of my life and listen to that small soft voice calling me the Beloved, I know that there is nothing to fear and that dying is the greatest act of love, the act that leads me into the eternal embrace of my God whose love is everlasting" (28:110–11).

The death of people close to him affected Nouwen profoundly. His spiritual reflections on these events produced several books concerned directly with death.

And what about Nouwen himself? It happened suddenly. The roads were slick. Everyone advised him to stay at home, but still he went out, on foot. A delivery van hit him, the outside mirror shoved into his side. What at first appeared to be a serious bruise turned out to be massive internal bleeding in the spleen. It was discovered in the nick of time and for a while he was in critical condition. Would he survive an operation to remove the spleen? "Somewhere, deep in me, I sensed that my life was in real danger. And so I let myself enter into a place I had never been before: the portal of death" (26:34).[59] Then wonderful things began to happen. During this process he underwent a near-death experience: "What I experienced was an intensely personal presence, a presence that pushed all my fears aside and said, 'Come, don't be afraid. I love you'" (26:35). He knew with certainty that it was Jesus, and in him the whole universe was present. "This experience was the realization of my oldest and deepest desires. Since the first moment of consciousness, I have had the desire to be with Jesus. Now I felt his presence in a most tangible way, as if my whole life had come together and I was being enfolded in love. The homecoming had a real quality of return, a return to the womb of God" (26:37–38). After the operation he slowly began to recover, and the single great question that remained was, "Why am I alive; why wasn't I found ready to enter into the house of God?" (26:50). Nouwen sought the answer in a deeper understanding of his vocation: "What I learned about dying is that I am called to die for others" (26:51).

Resurrection and Eternal Life

For many people, if not for most, death is a fearful giant hole in the distance, the literal end of everything, a mortal blow that even now casts its great shadow before us, paralyzing us. It is this paralysis that obstructs so much joy in the here and now and blocks our attention to others. So if dying people can demonstrate that for them death is not the end, this creates space and breathing room for those who have been close observers at their bedside. "The dying have the unique opportunity to set free those whom they leave behind.... In this perspective, life is a long journey of preparation — of preparing oneself to truly die for others. It is a series of little deaths in which we are asked to release many forms of clinging and to move increasingly from needing others to living for them" (26:52–53).

In the difficult time after his accident, Nouwen had a momentary experience of the pure presence of unconditional love. He said that this taught him henceforth to speak more from eternity than from "reality that passes away." "Having touched eternity, it seems to me impossible to point toward it as though it were not already here" (26:59). For Nouwen, this eternity was closely connected with the presence of Christ himself. Passing through death meant for him an encounter, a lifelong expectation that now would be fulfilled. Faith is always faith in the resurrection. But you can't prove anything with this "doctrine," "nor is it something to use to reassure people" (31:108). Theological doctrines are not generally operative truths; they must always be experienced, embodied, and appropriated. Nouwen was always very attentive in this matter. Only then can something as great as the resurrection be wholeheartedly believed and fully assented to. "The resurrection doesn't answer any of our curious questions about life after death, such as, How will it be? How will it look? But it does reveal to us that, indeed, love is stronger than death. After that revelation, we must remain silent, leave the whys, wheres, hows, and whens behind, and simply trust" (31:109).

Nouwen's thoughts about "eternal life" are even heavier with meaning. He confessed that for a long time he had seen eternal life as something for later, after this life. "But the older I become, the less interest my 'afterlife' holds for me. Worrying not only about tomorrow, next year, and the next decade, but even about the next life seems a false preoccupation. Wondering how things will be for me after I die seems, for the most part, a distraction. When my clear goal is the eternal life, that life must be reachable right now, where I am, because eternal life is life in and with God, and God is where I am here and now" (33:69). For those who can live this way — and living this way, a life with God in the here and now, is the heart of Christian spirituality — the dividing line between death and life disappears. "When our heart understands this divine truth, we are living the spiritual life" (33:70).

"We are sent into this world for a short time to say — through the joys and pains of our clocktime — the great 'Yes' to the love that has been given to us and in so doing return to the One who sent us with that 'Yes' engraved on our hearts. Our death thus becomes the moment of return. But our death can be this only if our whole life has been a journey back to the One from whom we come and who calls us the Beloved. There is such confusion about the idea of a life 'hereafter,' or 'the eternal life.' Personally, I do believe deeply in the eternal life, but not simply as a life after our physical death. It is only when we have claimed for ourselves the life of God's Spirit during the many moments of our 'chronology' that we expect death to be the door to the fullness of life. Eternal life is not some great surprise that comes unannounced at the end of our existence in time; it is, rather, the full revelation of what we have been and have lived all along. Death is the portal to the fullness of life" (28:109).

In conclusion, what is starkly evident in Nouwen's concern about death is the absence of any indictment of death, that death is an intruder which infects and embitters life, that death in fact does not belong in a good life. In Nouwen you do not find that struggle that is carried on by people who finally must admit that death has won, but who fight against it tooth and nail. Just look at the total humiliation of people with cancer and AIDS. Why? Why? is the question that burns in every heart, to be read in every eye, questions that are a major concern for pastoral care. Nouwen does not ignore these questions, but he turns them around, makes them gentle, lays them before the face of the Eternal One. To-day, when death ravages so many lives with such virulence — and this brings us back to the beginning of this chapter — Nouwen's spiritually faithful vision of death is extraordinarily important. Because before we know it, death pulls a fast one and holds our lives in check; every creative human expression is nipped in the bud and all efforts on behalf of the needy are crushed. It must be said that Nouwen's vision is a great task, a lifelong search. It demands an ever greater measure of surrender, of being taken where you do not want to go (John 21:18, see also chapter 20 below).

Part 3

SPIRITUALITY AND ETHICS

– 15 –

INTIMACY AND SOLIDARITY

Political and social affairs, which make up the substance of our everyday existence, and the affairs of the spiritual life, often seem like two mutually exclusive realities. The world around us is harsh and merciless. From the front pages of the newspapers and television news pictures a fierce world invades our living rooms. We are all little pawns in society's power games. Human lives scarcely count; hunger, violence, corruption, and discrimination are the order of the day. Money rules more than ever and puts people in second place. We have been made slaves of the almighty dollar.

The choice before us in such a situation is to flee "the cruel world" and leave it behind us. Even if we find it more or less necessary to "play the game" on society's battlefield, where do we go for breathing room? If the world and all that's in it holds us so firmly in its grip, where then is our freedom of movement?

There is none, many say, and so they then take refuge in platitudes and cynicism. The world? It will never change. People? Don't have too high an opinion of them, you can see what damage they've done, and you know all there is to know about yourself! This cynicism seems to be the sickness of our time; it's a deadly spiral that leads to intense darkness. Therefore another means of escape is created for people, inviting them to go around with their heads in the clouds so they no longer can see what's happening on the earth. When you're involved in spirituality and the spiritual life, you always run the risk of practicing it far from everyday life. You select a storm-free zone where gentle strength has free rein. You exchange the cold shivering world for the warm woolen blanket of spirituality. This highly exalted realm takes precedence over the lower regions where — according to this reasoning — we are all unfortunately forced to remain a bit longer. The divine is played against the human.

It has become clear in the previous two sections of this book that a Christian spirituality such as Nouwen proposes does not accord with these two means of escape, neither with the secular form (cynicism) nor with the Christian form (unearthly spirituality). In the following paragraphs I want to discuss this further. I want to show that his spirituality is deeply imbued with ethics, that it possesses a strong twofold quality of intimacy and solidarity. On the other hand, I want to show how fragile that connection is in his work, and that there are also tendencies that threaten to dissolve his spirituality.

Personal, Not Private

Nouwen's books demonstrate a strong involvement with the world. Whenever he brings himself into his writings, we can also see the political and social context of those particular years looming up. Many political ups and downs pass in review, but in a very special way, in a way that is quite different from what we are accustomed to in the church and theology. And that is precisely what makes his writings so exciting. Let me put it this way: Nouwen's way of looking at the world scene is not analytical but meditative or contemplative. He does not use rational analysis to line up all the facts in a row in order to propound an ethical position. Not that this is unacceptable or unimportant, but for that kind of specific analysis there are others available. Ethicists, politicians, and sociologists are the ones who investigate these matters. Nouwen was eager to become acquainted with their analyses, but his own interest began from another angle, a personal and religious angle.

First the personal angle. Right from the beginning in his first books he emphasized that the personal has universal dimensions. "Ultimately, I believe that what is most personal is also the most universal" (3:7). This statement has been frequently repeated and originally came from Carl Rogers. Nouwen proposed that the pastoral work of ministers consists of "offering your own life-experience to your fellow man and, as Paul Simon sings, to lay yourself down like a bridge over troubled water. I am not saying that you should talk about yourself, your personal worries, your family, your youth, your illnesses, or your hang-ups. That has nothing to do with availability. That is only playing a narcissistic game with your own idiosyncrasies. No, I mean that a preacher is called to experience life to such a depth that the meteorologist, the storekeeper, the farmer, and the laborer will all one day or another realize that he is touching places where their own lives also really vibrate, and in this way he allows them to become free to let the Word of God do its redemptive work. Because, as Carl Rogers says: 'What is most personal is most general' " (4:38).

These words were written in 1971. The 1960s were barely over. Certainly in the progressive Christian circles where Nouwen felt at home, a great deal of attention (too much perhaps?) was being paid to a socially engaged Christianity. Yes, there's a need for such a development, Nouwen argued, and he participated in it fully, but don't turn the Gospel into a daily newspaper or a television news report. Go beyond that and bring people to a place within and close to themselves, where everything social resonates with the personal.

"If any criticism can be made of the sixties, it is not that protest was meaningless but that it was not deep enough, in the sense that it was not rooted in the solitude of the heart. When only our minds and hands work together we quickly become dependent on the results of our actions and tend to give up when they do not materialize. In the solitude of the heart we can truly listen to the pains of the world because there we can recognize them not as strange and unfamiliar pains, but as pains that are indeed our own. There we can see that what is most universal is most personal and that indeed nothing human is strange to us" (8:41).

Please note that the personal to which Nouwen is referring is not the same as people's privacy, their private lives. Private life is gossip, rumor, it is secretively peeking through the keyhole in search of things that are not meant for other ears and eyes. Personal matters are existential matters, relevant matters, things that touch one's life and in this sense are public and open — just as the God of the Bible is a personal God who is openly looking for people with his highly unique story. "God is not a private God. The God who dwells in our inner sanctuary is also the God who dwells in the inner sanctuary of each human being" (33:22). It is here that Nouwen wanted to lead people; he wanted them to view the world and themselves from this central human core, to see the things that approach us not merely with the eyes of the world, but to learn to look at both the outside *and* the inside with the eyes of God. "One could call it the 'prophetic' vision: looking at people and this world through the eyes of God" (29:15). This is possible because God lives in us and has made a dwelling place in each of us. The personal approach also has spiritual and religious dimensions. The next section deals with this: God's path to us, God's movement toward each person's intimate region which is the source of our solidarity with the other.

Upward and Downward Mobility

With the dual concepts "upward mobility" and "downward mobility" Nouwen sketches the dynamic (and rivalry) that take place between God and humanity. People have the remarkable tendency to search for things by moving upward. They want fame; they're always after more. But there is something strange in this upward human striving. The higher they seek, the more they become alienated from themselves. This self-seeking is at the root of many of society's disasters. It is a devilish power that eagerly seduces us. Just as in the biblical story, the great adversary and sunderer (the *diabolos*, the devil) wants to tempt Jesus: be efficient and useful, to exercise power, and to do sensational things (33:100).

In numerous places Nouwen discusses this upward striving, this powerful attraction to have more, better, and higher. It is striking that he seldom illustrates this upward mobility in social terms, but he keeps completely in line with his own personal ethic. He seems to be saying, just look at people and their human activity, just look at me, and you can see how society is put together. "Everything in me wants to move upward" (23:154). Nouwen felt this drive toward efficiency, power, and sensational accomplishments most starkly during his short period at Harvard University. Young people are crammed through this very prestigious institution and prepared for a society that places enormous value on fame, public honor, and esteem. He couldn't stand it. Just back from Latin America, this was certainly the other extreme. At Daybreak, by living and working amid handicapped people he finally found what he was searching for. "So, here I am in my new surroundings. I may say that the contrast between my university life and my life here in L'Arche is greater than I realized at the outset. The contrast isn't so much between intelligent students and mentally handicapped people as in the 'ascending' style of the university and the 'descending' style of L'Arche. You might say that at Yale and Harvard they're principally interested in upward mobility, whereas here they believe in the importance of downward mobility. That's the radical difference; and I notice in myself how difficult it is to change direction on the ladder" (22:41).

Downward mobility is the movement of the kingdom of God, from God to us, which is visible in Jesus. On their own, human beings are apparently incapable of coming up with the idea of searching among the lowest, the little ones and the oppressed. It is this "downward mobility" that lives in every story from the Bible and is then passed down. Put even more strongly, it is just this movement that makes the Gospel good news: God comes down, disturbing and thwarting our human striving — and saving us. Nouwen's ethic is a kenotic ethic — that is, we are invited to go the self-denying, self-emptying way of Christ (which is the meaning of kenosis, see Philippians 2:7). This is all completely opposed to what we find in ourselves and our society. "Downward mobility with Jesus goes radically against my inclinations, against the advice of the world surrounding me, and against the culture of which I am a part" (23:154).

Ethics and Community

But there's danger lurking, for in following the downward mobility of Jesus the focus can get redirected back to ourselves. That is, we may secretly begin beating our breasts for doing so many good works. It's a very subtle situation. Everyone who is socially active (both in the church and outside it) recognizes this temptation: that one's social commitment, however good and valuable, is really just an opportunity to stroke one's own ego. Nouwen saw through this temptation. "My whole life I have been surrounded by well-meaning encouragement to go 'higher up,' and the most-used argument was: 'You can do so much good there, for so many people'" (33:101).

Here is where I see Nouwen's great contribution to the many (often crippling) ethical debates that are going on in the church and elsewhere. He advocates an ethical-spiritual approach, namely, that we must break the habit of acting out of the profit-and-results mode of thinking (that's still "upward mobility"). Not that it is unimportant to attain results (no war, no hunger, no suffering). On the contrary. But if we want to arrive at that point, then selflessness and humility are necessary. Indeed, isn't it true that actions and social plans often run aground because human vanity and self-interest block any real chance for commitment?[60] A figure such as St. Francis is an example of another way of acting. "He revealed not only his own nakedness but also the nakedness of all people before God" (16:68). Such a religious-ethical attitude changes the face of the world. But we also know that even during Francis's lifetime, this poverty movement was severely afflicted by quarrels and ambition.

This spirituality is being practiced in the midst of all the political bickering in a world that is often balanced on the edge of the abyss. "It is of great importance to see the inner connection between intimacy and solidarity. If we fail to recognize this connection our spirituality will become either privatized or narrowly activist and will no longer reflect the full beauty of living in God's house" (20:43–44). Highly relevant efforts (acts of service/ diakonia) can be exercised from this perspective in a whole host of small- or large-scale social activities. This helps alleviate the great tensions that often plague personal and social affairs. "Here we are touching the profound spiritual truth that service is an expression of the search for God and not just of the desire to bring about individual or social change" (16:31). Seen in this light, it's sometimes even better to give up some of our many activities because they may cause us to lose our vision of God and to grow deaf to the joy within us. "When we are committed to do God's will and not our own we soon discover that much of what we do doesn't need to be done by us. What we are called to do are actions that bring us true joy and peace" (35:100).

It is only in community that this spirituality of solidarity really begins to take shape. There you discover that the world may not revolve around you alone. When you're by yourself it's difficult to maintain any kind of perspective. Spirituality seems to cry out for community. In community what is personal is expanded, without being lost in the collective. Here contact with the Eternal One is learned and practiced in prayer and struggle. "What do we really desire? As I try to listen to my own deepest yearning as well as the yearnings of others, the word that seems best to summarize the desire of the human heart is 'communion.' Communion means 'union with.' God has given us a heart that will remain restless until it has found full communion" (33:43).

This longing for community is a thread that runs through Nouwen's life. In the biographical part of this book I showed how urgently he searched for a place where the religious life can be sustained, gauged, criticized, and sheltered. Finally he found this community at L'Arche. "A human community" — that's what the church should be, for the church (as an institution) is also often affected by upward mobility. In the church it's more a matter of survival than living. It is striking that Nouwen seldom speaks about "the church."[61] The word he prefers is the "Christian community." Speaking about the church, with all its ailments and defects, distracts our attention from what is really important. It's not that he didn't want to be a "son of the church," or that he wanted to turn his back on it, but the church and everything that goes with it have to keep learning about community over and over again, in breaking and sharing. He writes about "bread and wine," the Eucharist, where personal religious experience is enriched and solidarity is learned. "The Christian community mediates between the suffering of the world and our individual responses to this suffering" (16:55). "In community, our lives become compassionate lives because in the way we live and work together, God's compassion becomes present in the midst of a broken world" (16:56–57).

Political Involvement?

I noted earlier that Nouwen approached issues much more from a social than a political viewpoint. There is a difference between them. The latter places more blame on the structures of society and deals more with the validity of political systems. Advocates of this approach claim that capitalistic and/or communistic structures enslave people and keep them inferior, that Money — or the Party — calls the shots. We do not find these kinds of analyses in Nouwen. During his Latin American period he came into full contact with them, but as we've seen he found these political theologies (usually Marxist-oriented) too insistent, too oblivious to concrete human beings.

Digression: Nouwen's Reception in the Netherlands and Flanders

The reception of a famous Dutchman who has sojourned elsewhere and has scarcely set foot in his own land is always fascinating. In order to focus in on these events, I would like to sketch very briefly my own development and the point at which Nouwen and I met. In this connection it is also important to refer back to chapter 4, about Nouwen's departure from the Netherlands and the implications of this move for his spirituality.

As was true of so many others in the late 1960s and early 1970s, my theological education was quite political, and up to the present day I have been politically and socially active in church-related social welfare work. As a Protestant minister I had never heard of Henri Nouwen. But even people in his own Catholic Church in the Netherlands barely knew him, and among those who did, at least in progressive church circles, he was regarded with skepticism. In Flanders it was not much different, except he already had many readers there. People saw him as a writer of pious, soft, typical American books that did not offer much to improve the world. And the fact that he was becoming fairly popular in conservative Catholic circles in the Netherlands and beyond — wasn't that proof enough?

In the summer of 1984 I met Nouwen for the first time in the town of Holland(!) in the state of Michigan during a meeting of more or less progressive Christian communities, among which, for example, was the Sojourners community of Washington, D.C. This encounter, taking place during a very socially conscious yet pious convention, was a revelation for me in the sense that Nouwen's spirituality was starting to deepen my political involvement step by step. I was learning that solidarity without its fruitful partner, intimacy (political and mystical), becomes watered down. This is a learning process that I have since tried to bring into theological discussions in the Netherlands and Flanders. I introduced Nouwen's work in many different settings.

But times changed with the approach of the "fin de siècle." The social results of our actions, on which we had pinned such high hopes, failed to materialize. It doesn't look as though the world is going to improve very much during our lifetime, and probably not during our children's lifetimes either. So we've got to draw water from other wells. It was these wells, already dried up for many, that Nouwen tapped anew in search of the living water that could quicken our cold hearts and thirsty throats. Statistics show that Nouwen is the most widely read writer in the English-speaking world in the area of Christian spirituality. In his own country, the Netherlands, this is not yet true. But this is gradually changing. Considering the spiritual climate in Western Europe during the last few decades, it simply wasn't possible for him to make a "breakthrough." But things have changed, and I see the tide turning. Conservative believers with an itch to restore the church to what it used to be are going to discover that he is not merely the pious Nouwen who comforts the soul, a faithful son of Holy Mother Church, but that his spirituality is socially renewing and radical. And skeptical progressive believers are becoming more receptive. Their political radicalism, which admittedly is something that they do not find in Nouwen as such, is freed from narrowness and pedantry in Nouwen's approach. Suddenly there's more room, room for encounters and for renewing energy. And all this is taking place because the Eternal One is not going to abandon the work already begun.

When Time Touches Eternity

Did Nouwen ever express himself about the political and social organization of society? Yes, but I've only run across it in one place in his work. In *With Open Hands* (3) he came close when he wrote about prayer and revolution: "You are Christian only so long as you look forward to a new world, so long as you constantly pose critical questions to the society you live in" (3:126). Much later, just after returning from Latin America and after his first contact with Jean Vanier, he wrote during a stay in Trosly: "We need a new economic order beyond socialism and capitalism which makes justice for all its goal" (20:113). On the same pages he speaks about "academics of peace, ministries of peace, and peacekeeping forces" (20:113), all this contained within "a global spirituality in which the demands of the Gospel guide not only the behavior of individuals but of nations as well" (20:111). But it would be too far afield to elaborate on this political vision, what I would call a third way between capitalism and communism.[62] I read into this the inspiration of Dag Hammarskjöld (1905–61) and his commitment to making the United Nations a genuine and firm organization for peace. His *Markings* demonstrate that this is an impossible task without a spiritual anchor.[63]

To sum up: Nouwen expressed a personal, spiritually charged ethic that followed the radical downward mobility of Jesus into the heart of our world. In the Christian community this movement of solidarity is celebrated, professed, and lived out. Herein lies his ethical primacy; the analysis of political facts follows only at a distance. An example of this last point: When the Berlin Wall tottered and fell at the end of 1989, he was eager to follow these tense days firsthand in order to experience "the radical changes that were taking place in Europe at the beginning of a new decade. I didn't go." Where did he go? To Lourdes! Why at this historical moment did he decide it was time to go there? "At this moment in history — my own as well as that of the world — I have to go to the very center of being: the center where time touches eternity, where earth and heaven meet, where God's Word becomes human flesh, where death and immortality embrace" (30:31).

– 16 –

COMPASSION, CARING, FREEDOM

That which is true for the key spiritual concepts in part 2 — that they are not concerned with abstract theories — is also true for the ethical dimensions of Nouwen's books. He was not interested in formulating ethical principles; rather he wanted to demonstrate what really happens to human beings when they learn to look at this world and themselves through the eyes of God. When people learn to see Jesus in the life of the other, they change. They become compassionate, caring, and ultimately free people. "Compassion" is the basic stance. "Caring" is what literally develops out of compassion. And freedom is the beckoning perspective within which this takes place. These three terms appear frequently in Nouwen's books; they form the heart of his spiritual ethics. At the risk of schematizing too much I treat them here briefly.

Compassion

In 1982 a book appeared which was wholly devoted to this theme, *Compassion: A Reflection on the Christian Life* (16). Nouwen wrote it with two of his colleagues. I find it his most theological book. Reflections on spiritual concepts are more firmly grounded here than anywhere else. The hymn to Christ in the Letter to the Philippians (2:6–11) forms the biblical framework for his observations. The basic meaning of this quintessential Nouwen word is defined right at the outset. "The word *compassion* is derived from the Latin words *pati* and *cum,* which together mean 'to suffer with.' Compassion asks us to go where it hurts, to enter into places of pain, to share in brokenness, fear, confusion, and anguish. Compassion challenges us to cry out with those in misery, to mourn with those who are lonely, to weep with those in tears. Compassion requires us to be weak with the weak, vulnerable with the vulnerable, and powerless with the powerless. Compassion means full immersion in the condition of being human" (16:4). In this very eloquent passage, all of the words and concepts that are included come together to form to the word "compassion" and to impart a cadence to his work.

So compassion can be seen as a moral designation that helps humanity along, but we as human beings are not all that eager to enter into the brokenness of this world. On the contrary, we would much rather keep our distance. "Compassion is not among our most natural responses. We are pain-avoiders and we consider anyone who feels attracted to suffering abnormal, or at least very unusual" (16:4). So how can people be compassionate when their natural inclination is to shrink from and run away from compassion? As a possible answer to this question, Nouwen once again addresses the human "inner sanctuary," that pivotal spot where God and humanity meet. "When you are able to create a lonely place in the middle of your actions and concerns, your successes and failures slowly can lose some of their power over you. For then your love for this world can merge with a compassionate understanding of its illusions. Then your serious engagement can merge with an unmasking smile. Then your concern for others can be motivated more by their needs than your own. In short: then you can care. Let us therefore live our lives to the fullest but let us not forget to once in a while get up long before dawn to leave the house and go to a lonely place" (7:26).

Caring, Being Careful

It would not be overstating the case to say that all of Nouwen's passion is directed at making himself and others sensitive to the

secret contained in the act of caring. He calls it "our precious gift
of care" (31:104). When he deals with concrete human intimacy
in his books, this word pops up continuously. According to him,
the word "care" comes from the Gothic "kara," which means
"to grieve, to experience sorrow, to cry out with" (7:34). There
is nothing condescending in this. It is not the case that the one
who cares should possess and give to the other something that
the other does not have. On the contrary, we must first recognize
that we stand with empty hands at the side of someone who is
seriously ill or dying, or who is undergoing great suffering. "The
friend who cares makes it clear that whatever happens in the external world, being present to each other is what really matters"
(7:35). Nouwen noted these words not as just so much pastoral
wisdom, but as words born out of his concrete encounters with
the elderly (*Aging*, 6), the dying (*Our Greatest* Gift, 31), AIDS
patients, and handicapped people.

During the years at L'Arche, the words "compassion" and
"care" had to be tested for their interior value and tenability
more than ever before, and not by another person but by Nouwen
himself! He asked himself whether this beautiful yet highly theoretical language really holds water. Indeed, these were concepts
that were no longer being spoken or taught at the universities
of Yale and Harvard, and they were no longer "appropriate" in
Latin America, where in his heart of hearts he did not feel at
home. "Very few stones remain unturned. Care, compassion, love
for neighbor, promise, commitment, and faithfulness...I turned
and turned these concepts in my mind and heart, and sometimes
it felt as though the spiritual house I had built up over the years
was now proving to be made of cardboard and ready to go up in
flames" (23:222).

Freedom and Joy

So does this mean that the whole house of cards is doomed to
collapse? Nouwen doesn't pull any punches for his readers, now
that it's come this far. He urges us to look with him. For in times

of enormous spiritual turbulence — and you can almost hear it crying out — he places the question where it ultimately belongs, where all the Christian mystics and spiritual leaders have taught us to locate the question, where the only answer according to them can be found: in falling and rising again. This is the whole thing in a nutshell: "The most radical challenge came out of the question, 'Is Jesus truly enough for you, or do you keep looking for others to give you your sense of worth?'" (23:222). If I hold back something of myself and for myself and then strike a nice little bargain with God and Jesus, my spirituality is nothing but smoke and my ethics nothing but hot air.

This is the question that sets Christian spirituality balancing on the edge of the abyss. All too many fall into the abyss and, against their better judgment, they are challenged by the Eternal One to start all over again, right from the top, hoping for the best. That's what the spiritual life is all about; that's how Nouwen wanted to write about it, as an interior struggle that ultimately offers freedom. "Free at last" — that is the vision that Martin Luther King Jr. gave humanity with his life and his death. "Freedom belongs to the core of the spiritual life; not just the freedom which releases us from forces that want to oppress us, but the freedom also to forgive others, to serve them, and to form a new bond of fellowship with them. In short, the freedom to love and to work for a free world" (22:18–19).

The words "compassion," "caring," and "freedom" serve as a triptych of Nouwen's ethics. Together they contribute to the great evangelical process of healing, the healing of the world and of humanity. These are not static images that reproduce this beautiful painting. There are other visible elements as well, in all sorts of tints and colors: hospitality and friendship, for example. But above all there is joy. Just when you think that the triptych has become too dark, that these human activities seem too much like obligations, then the light color of joy jumps out at you. Indeed, we so often experience the world as a dark planet that we are in danger of forgetting that the earth always turns to its sunny side. I don't think I'm going too far when I say that Nouwen's ethic is encircled by a deep joy. "Joy is the secret gift of compassion"

(33:103). This joy reaches us through those for whom we put ourselves out. I have something for the other, certainly for the other who suffers, only if I first dare to receive his or her gift. This conversion is of vital importance because it lets us escape from the heaviness of existence and gradually leads us into the house of God's love. "The joy that compassion brings is one of the best-kept secrets of humanity. It is a secret known to only a very few people, a secret that has to be rediscovered over and over again" (33:102).

Part 4

THEOLOGICAL
INSIGHTS

– 17 –

CLOWNING THEOLOGY

Whoever writes, speaks, and preaches, using words from the world of faith and religion, is always somehow busy with theology. Theology originates in the context of the very far-flung Christian faith tradition and is in ongoing conversation with those who have been developing theological insights, who have pursued new paths, or who have chosen to remain outside the appropriate tradition. No one theologizes in a vacuum. Even those who will have nothing to do with theology ("all that scholarly business," they protest), are still doing theology as soon as they write or utter just one word about belief. Theology is a "branch of learning" that critically looks and listens whenever people or churches broach the subject of God, Jesus, church, or humanity. This is how I understand theology: as a critical pursuit and inquiry about the numerous statements and fragments of statements that are being made in the context of belief. For an enormous number of claims are being made in the realm of faith, church, and religion. I am aware that a "definition" of theology, if it is even possible, is enough in and of itself to provoke a theological discussion. For where is the reflection's point of departure, on what criteria do I base any possible judgment? These are scholarly, theoretical questions that I do not intend to address within the scope of this book. It would do too much harm to the liveliness of a writer such as Nouwen.

What I do want to say with these introductory words is that Nouwen also "produced" theology. There are theological strains in his works as well as a certain development. His way of thinking proceeds from presuppositions in which particular images of

God and humanity are operative. He also makes theological decisions which may or may not deviate from familiar aspects of
Roman Catholicism. Reflection on Nouwen's theology is therefore possible, but it's also necessary, because there's a lot of
theology buzzing and resounding in the forty written works that
he penned. Since the purpose of this book does not allow a close
examination of all the religious themes, I will confine myself to a
few broad lines.

Theology as System and Theology as Art

We have seen that Henri seldom discoursed on systematic theology, but seized opportunities in and around his own life to write
about. Theology was presumed and then relinquished in order
further to investigate the described experiences in a meditative
(theological) fashion. Actually, he primarily wanted to stay as far
away as possible from what "the" church or "the" faith says. It is
church and professed religion, after all, that can stand in the way
of human experiences.

Nouwen's procedure does not make it easy to reflect on this
aspect of his work. At first glance he seems to jump from one
subject to another, dealing with almost all the ups and downs that
a person can go through in life. In part 2 we noted a few central
spiritual concepts. So now the question is what theological lines
we can discover there.

At first it must be said that they are indeed lines, rough
sketches. Nouwen's thinking is never finished, and it does not lend
itself to ever being described as a complete whole; it's too creative
for that, too dynamic, always on the move. He was not interested
in highly disciplined thought. Rather he resisted theology as a system; it had wreaked too much havoc already, both ecclesiastically
and personally.

It's an "art" to photograph this "free bird" in flight, to let
him fly freely and not to clip his wings. This theological "photograph" has to radiate the same dynamism as the bird itself. For
this is how Nouwen wanted to understand theology, as a kind

of art. Theology must reveal an artistry that gives it wings. This provides space for a free fall, as with the Flying Rodleighs, the trapeze artists who made such a lasting impression on Nouwen. Their technique, their training, their materials, their bodies, their mutual solidarity, this whole array (their "theology") is meant to serve that one leap, that "salto vitale," the religious experience.

Here in a nutshell is the change that Nouwen wanted to bring about in theology: he wanted theology to be of service to this "art," to this spirituality. He realized in this that he was touching the nerve of theological and church structures. Although in the beginning it may have seemed that as a professor he wanted to effect this change on a scholarly level, he quickly came to the discovery that his strength did not lay in the scholarly realm. No, the turnabout would have to take place in himself! This did not begin as a preconceived notion, with Nouwen declaring "now I'm going to work on my spirituality." It came about spontaneously, something he gradually discovered in himself and others. His books show this process, this spiritual journey and pilgrimage. It is a movement "from...to": from illusion to prayer in *Reaching Out* (8), from the house of anxiety to the house of love in *Lifesigns* (20). I would like to call this Nouwen's spiritual methodology; this is how he wrote his books. And this is how he saw the human life fitting together, alternating between extremes in order to be found somewhere in the middle by the Eternal One.

Nouwen's first books were still quite theological. After all, he wrote them while he was instructing future ministers. Just as theology must be artistic, so he liked to describe ministers as clowns. *Intimacy* (1), *Creative Ministry* (4), *The Wounded Healer* (5), *The Living Reminder* (10), and *Clowning in Rome* (11) were all written during the Yale period as books for pastors. Ministers have a lot to unlearn; their dogmatic and ethical jackets are too tight. "Often it seems that we who study or teach theology find ourselves entangled in such a complex network of discussions, debates, and arguments about God and 'God-issues' that a simple conversation with God or a simple presence to God has become practically impossible" (13:47). Theology as a system has to make room for a "clowning" theology. Only then do pastor and believers come into contact with the heart of theology, the experience of the Eternal One. "God is not simply Someone whom we discover in our research. Someone about whom we preach our clear scientific discoveries from the pulpit. How can we possibly expect anyone to find real nurture, comfort, and consolation from a prayer life that taxes the mind beyond its limits and adds one more exhausting activity to the many already scheduled ones?" (13:74).

Such sharp tones are rare in Nouwen; either the heart starts beating in the presence of such questions or the whole business is totally lifeless! Once at Genesee when he had to listen to a theological lecture he sighed, "Listening to the lectures reawakened in me all my seminary feelings. I kept saying to myself, 'How interesting, how fascinating, how insightful' — and at the same time I said to myself, 'So what? What do all these words about God the Father, the Son, and the Spirit have to do with me here and now?' As soon as I step outside the circle of his terminology, which is very familiar to me, the whole level of discourse seems extremely alienating" (9:150).

Dogmatic padding hinders a free spiritual experience of faith, and if the spiritual leaders of a church (pastors, bishops, religious, and others) cannot break loose from this practice, then they themselves prevent the development of the vitally important community. His penetrating book *Creative Ministry* (4) was an impassioned plea to make the practical areas of theology more spiritual. "It is painful to realize that very few ministers are able to offer the rich mystical tradition of Christianity as a source of rebirth for the generation searching for new life in the midst of the debris of a faltering civilization" (4:114). This is especially necessary right now because "we are approaching a period of an increased search for spirituality that is the experience of God in this very moment of our existence" (4:115).

Theology was certainly very important for Nouwen, but "seminaries and divinity schools must lead theology students into an ever-growing communion with God, with each other, and with their fellow human beings. Theological education is meant to form our whole person toward an increasing conformity with the

mind of Christ so that our way of praying and our way of believing will be one" (13:47). In this way he wanted to restore
theology's original purpose and meaning. "The original meaning
of the word 'theology' was 'union with God in prayer.' Today theology has become one academic discipline alongside many others,
and often theologians are finding it hard to pray. But for the future of Christian leadership it is of vital importance to reclaim the
mystical aspect of theology so that every word spoken, every advice given, and every strategy developed can come from a heart
that knows God intimately" (25:30).

Mystical Theology

When we open ourselves to these points of view, we can say that
in the context of modern theological trends Nouwen's choice was
for a mystical theology. This is the way theology was regarded
and practiced in the past, when pure analytical reason was not
yet predominant but was subordinate and subservient to the mysteries of faith. Nouwen did not favor an uncritical return to those
bygone days. He felt that that was what some of the evangelical and pentecostal churches are doing, the ones that are growing
in influence in the Christian Coalition in the United States. He
wanted to take into account and involve the modern and postmodern insights from the last century and the related human
experiences.[64]

In his first book Nouwen wrote an essay that I believe presents
the program for his later ideas. It breathes the open atmosphere of
Vatican II. Here he takes up his theological position and sets the
tone. Here, even at this early stage, we recognize the author who
was to come. In many keys, timbres, and modifications he would
compose variations on this "theme." "A deeper understanding of
the incarnation leads to a rethinking of the humanity of God.
More and more it has become clear that God reveals Himself
to man through man and his world and that a deeper understanding of human behavior leads us to a deeper understanding
of God. The new insights of psychology, sociology, anthropology

and so forth are no longer feared as possible threats to the super-natural God, but more as an invitation to theological reflection on the new insights and understandings. Vatican II strongly supported this humanization of the church, and the new theology was a great encouragement to mobilize all the human potentialities in the different levels of human life as being the most authentic way to understand the voice of God to His people. The new theology was 'discovered' by a deeper understanding of the createdness of the world, by discerning that there is a task of Christian secularization" (1:74).

To put it in sharper theological focus: God has entered into the reality of creation (incarnation and downward mobility). Although separate from creation, God is nevertheless fully joined with it. Precisely because reality (humanity and the world) is from God, created by God, then nothing in or about that reality is alien to God. That opens tremendous perspectives and possibilities. Indeed, this God-given creation asks, as it were, for fulfillment, for a complete humanity (ethics, part 3). Creation waits and points to Christ; in Christ God has turned toward us with his Very Best and has shown us the Divine Face. We have been looked upon and loved by that Face. Even though these theological sentences sound somewhat abstract, the main point for Nouwen was in the faith experience of being seen and knowing that one is loved.

Now then, mystical theology, with contemplation at its heart, does not stop at dogmatic formulations and scholarly analyses, but desires to help people in this knowledge of the divine experience. An example that Nouwen used can demonstrate this. It is about the artistic skills of a sculptor who already sees a work of art in a rough block of marble. Our reality and our lives within it can be compared with that rough block of marble to which something must happen. "The art of sculpture is, first of all, the art of seeing. In one block of marble, Michelangelo saw a loving mother carrying her dead son on her lap.... The image of the sculptor offers us a beautiful illustration of the relationship between contemplation and ministry. To contemplate is to *see*, and to minister is to *make visible*; the contemplative life is a life with a vision, and the life of ministry is a life in which this vision is revealed to others" (11:87–88).

The mystical (contemplative) life is a life in which we are continually moving from dark reticence to transparency (Thomas Merton). So mystical theology is highly ethical; the sight, the vision, what you see in the marble must be carved out. Without vision, our activity (our ministry) is empty and fruitless; you carve, but in a rather hit-or-miss fashion. Without activity the vision is not visible; we and the world remain as an uncarved piece of marble. With these notions Nouwen gives a contemporary touch to the desert father Evagrius Ponticus (c. 345–99). "Evagrius calls contemplation a *theoria physike,* which means a vision (*theoria*) of the nature of things (*physike*)" which requires a spiritual discipline of the *praktikos* (11:88). "The contemplative looks not so much around things but through them into their center. Through their center he discovers the world of spiritual beauty that is more real, has more density, more mass, more energy, and greater intensity than physical matter. In effect, the beauty of physical matter is a reflection of its inner content. Contemplation is a response to a world that is built in this fashion. That is why the Greek fathers, who were great contemplatives, are known as the dioretic fathers. *Diorao* means to see into, to see through. . . . I really must enter that 'other side,' the quiet, rhythmic, solid side of life, the deep solid stream moving underneath the restless waves of my sea" (9:20–21).

Out of these theological insights emerges an active, dynamic God who as the First Love is continually busy creating and incarnating in order to shape us in the divine image and likeness. "The Lord is at the center of all things and yet in such a quiet, unobtrusive, elusive way. He lives with us, even physically, but not in the same physical way that other elements are present to us" (9:19).[65] This sentence is not meant to be a definition of God, but is immediately held up to experience. "God is close but often too close to experience. God is closer to me than I am to myself and, therefore, no subject for feelings or thoughts. . . . The experience of God's presence is not void of pain. But the pain is so deep that you do not want to miss it since it is in this pain that the joy of

God's presence can be tasted. This seems close to nonsense except in the sense that it is beyond sense and, therefore, hard to capture within the limits of human understanding" (9:120–21). The initiative remains on God's side. "God should be sought, but we cannot find God. We can only be found by him" (9:116).

"I Can Say No More Than That..."

Did Nouwen have any doubts? Did he speak about this God with a certainty that was wholly beyond the feelings of many people in this postmodern culture? Can we still go along with a God who is present as a kind of stage set, hanging behind all of our activities and giving them direction? Isn't the experience of many people that of emptiness instead? Indeed, for some, Nouwen's visions were just too much, too certain — for his friend Fred, for example, to whom he tried to explain Christian spirituality (and the meaning of life) in *Life of the Beloved* (28). It did not work; Fred couldn't buy it. He gave up, just as Nouwen's nephew Marc gave up (22). We might have learned a lot about faith and theology in these times if Marc had responded to the letters his uncle sent him. Fred said: " 'Your words are based on many presuppositions that we don't share with you. You are not aware of how truly secular we are' " (28:115). Does Nouwen preach to the choir? Is his spirituality nothing but an in-house phenomenon meant for the Christian church alone? He admitted quite frankly to Fred the meaning of his writings: "These experiences are completely pervaded with the knowledge of God's presence" (28:117). And he did not consider it his task to convince him. "I feel within myself a deep-rooted resistance to proving anything to anybody. I don't want to say: 'I will show you that you need God to live a full life.' I can only say: 'For me, God is the one who calls me the Beloved, and I have a desire to express to others how I try to become more fully who I already am.' But beyond that I feel very poor and powerless.... At this moment, I can say no more than that" (28:117–18).

– 18 –

CHRIST, THE HEART OF GOD, HUMANITY, AND THE WORLD

Incarnation and Self-Emptying

The Christian tradition teaches us to speak "with two words." We tell our children to "speak with two words" when we want to instill in them a notion of politeness toward others, so that they say not only "thanks" but "thank you"; not only "hello," but "hello, ma'am." These good manners also apply to the Christian tradition. You cannot speak about God without Jesus. And the opposite is also true: you cannot speak about Jesus apart from the God of Israel. This mode of behavior, so simple and obvious at first glance, has greater implications than we usually suspect. But the language that is used to forge this belief into truth — the profession of faith and the catechism, for example — puts many people off. How then can this mystery, this heart of the Christian faith, be clearly presented and still be considered up to date? This is the not inconsequential problem that Nouwen takes up.[66]

In the last chapter the concept of incarnation came up briefly in a quote. God has become human, God-with-us. Now that this is so, we can also become fully human; "since God has become man, it is man who has the power to lead his fellow man to freedom" (5:71).[67] For Nouwen, this concentration on Christ is a basic aspect of all his thinking and writing. "The mystery of the Incarnation is that it has become possible to see God in and through Jesus Christ. Christ is the image of God" (11:78). Nouwen does not present this statement as an article of faith, for in contemplative prayer it can actually be experienced and known. "Contemplative prayer can be described as an imagining of Christ, a letting him enter fully into our consciousness so that he becomes the icon always present in our inner room" (11:78). He expresses it this way in the words of a prayer: "Dear Lord, help me keep my eyes on you. You are the incarnation of Divine Love, you are the expression of God's infinite compassion, you are the visible manifestation of God's holiness" (15:34).

This emphasis on the uniqueness of Christ in no sense means that God is being inadequately addressed. On the contrary, you might say that this is how God wants to be; we discover God in that downward mobility. In the parable of the prodigal son the description is very familiar. "But the father of the prodigal son is not concerned about himself. His long-suffering life has emptied him of his desires to keep in control of things. His children are his only concern, to them he wants to give himself completely, and for them he wants to pour out all of himself" (29:119–20).[68]

The incarnation resulted in one person, in *the* person Jesus. As a human person he encompassed all humanity by becoming the least, by emptying himself as a slave. The images from the hymn to Christ in Philippians 2 run like a thread through all of Nouwen's work. Incarnation and kenosis are a feature of all his notions of Christ. "Jesus emptied himself. He gave up a privileged position, a position of majesty and power, and assumed fully and without reservation a condition of total dependency. Paul's hymn of Christ does not ask us to look upward, away from our condition, but to look in our midst and discover God there" (16:25–26). These sentences are pregnant with meaning: "Latin America offers us the image of the suffering Christ" (18:31), and "Jesus is God who-suffers-with-us" (22:31).

A Damaged Icon

We see how an all too familiar and orthodox picture of Jesus becomes democratized, as it were — made tangible for everyone. Jesus is no longer the highly exalted king seen at a great distance, but he is close to us. In Christ God comes to us, suffers with us, and journeys with us in the caravan of our lives. The theology that developed after the Second World War did not leave Nouwen unaffected. This christology can be found in the chapters of the book *Letters to Marc about Jesus* (22): "Jesus: The Heart of Our Existence"; "Jesus: The God Who Sets Us Free"; "Jesus: The Compassionate God"; "Jesus: The Descending God"; "Jesus: The Loving God;" "Jesus: The Hidden God." Some of the section titles in earlier chapters reflect this once again. His key spiritual concepts (part 2), ethics (part 3), and theology (this part) all revolved around the One Name. "If you were to ask me point-blank, 'What does it mean to you to live spiritually?' I would have to reply, 'Living with Jesus at the center' " (22:7). Thus Nouwen understood theology as "thinking with the mind of Christ." That is real theological thinking (see 25:66). That is real personal thinking. "I am gradually discovering what it means to say that my sonship and the sonship of Jesus are one, that my return and the return of Jesus are one, that my home and the home of Jesus are one. There is no journey to God outside of the journey that Jesus made" (29:50).

This intimate, suffering Christ is pictured most penetratingly by Nouwen when he meditates on the icon of the Savior of Zvenigorod by Andrew Rublev (early fifteenth century). This icon has not survived history without a scratch. The image is seriously damaged; only the face of Christ is still visible. In the same way Christ lives with us, "a most tender human face, and eyes that penetrate the heart of God as well as every human heart. . . . A sad but still very beautiful face looks at us through the ruins of our world" (21:46).

L'Arche: The Broken Person and the Ministry of Jesus

The figure of Jesus lives among humanity, damaged and wounded. He is the wounded healer who in his downward mobility (incarnation) searches for broken people and shares in the brokenness of our existence. The L'Arche movement of Jean Vanier is such a place where wounded people live together. The mentally and often also physically handicapped people make up the core of the community. Around them are the others, their assistants. They live together in an impressive intimacy, and nowhere is it more deeply experienced how much the "healthy" are also wounded in body and soul and in need of a healer. At Daybreak Nouwen was the pastor of this group of people. It was in this physical environment that the concept of incarnation took on a much deeper meaning. Jean Vanier taught him "that L'Arche is built upon the body and not upon the word. This helps to explain my struggle in coming to L'Arche. Until now my whole life has been centered around the word: learning, teaching, reading, writing, speaking. Without the word, my life is unthinkable.... L'Arche, however, is built not on words, but on the body. The community of L'Arche is a community formed around the wounded bodies of handicapped people. Feeding, cleaning, touching, holding — this is what builds the community. Words are secondary. Most handicapped people have few words to speak, and many do not speak at all. It is the language of the body that counts most. 'The Word became flesh.' That is the center of the Christian message" (23:150–51).

For fourteen months at Daybreak Nouwen took on direct responsibility for Adam, a severely physically and mentally handicapped young man. From the long hours of caring, direct contact and making himself available he told Adam's story. "Out of this broken body and broken mind emerged a most beautiful human being offering me a greater gift than I would ever be able to offer him. It is hard for me to find adequate words for this experience, but somehow Adam revealed to me who he was and who I was and how we can love each other" (34/4:13–14).[69]

On February 13, 1996, Adam died at the age of thirty-four. "There are few people who have had as much influence on my life as Adam," Nouwen confessed.[70] In a full account of Adam's dying, his burial, and the reactions of the community, Nouwen writes: "During these past three days I have come to see more clearly than ever before that Adam was the living Christ among us."[71]

Adam, Man. *Nomen est omen.* The name is a sign. Adam's

name is a sign, and this became more and more true for Nouwen. It is true that in their brokenness living people, here and
now, point to the First among all humans, the second Adam. It
is Jesus himself.

The Human Heart: Point of Contact
Between God and Humanity

Is there a place where God and humanity touch? Is there a place
where heaven and earth meet? "I don't experience anything!" is
the anguished cry of many people today. There's no communication at all between God and me. There's no way that God can
exist. We hear these whispered words from Fred and Marc. Does
Nouwen do anything with these questions from modern secular
men and women? Does he get inside their skin? At least he makes
an attempt, but he himself admits that he can't discuss it, and
he refuses to proselytize. And theologizing, critical reflection, isn't
his strong suit either. What then? Well, just give it up. I have only
myself, he seems to say. I'll give an account of my religious experiences, and you must simply decide whether they mean anything
to you. Nouwen's books do mean something to many people. His
readers are uplifted, they feel personally addressed and carried
along by his moving narrative style. It touches their lives. This
personal faith experience mediates between faith and practice. In
this last section it all comes down to this: are the grand words of
"faith" and "spirituality," which he himself uses so much, nothing but words, or do they take root, quite literally, and become
embedded somewhere? And where might that be?

In Nouwen's writings I see this place of encounter steadily taking shape with sharper and more meaningful contours. It seems as
if the encounter with God becomes more present with the passing
of years. He talks about "a space within us where God dwells
and where we are invited to dwell with God. Once we come to
know that inner, holy place, a place more beautiful and precious
than any place we can travel to, we want to be there and be spiritually fed" (33:21). It is in this "inner sanctuary" that people

are slowly formed in the image of Christ. This has direct ethical consequences, because "the closer we come to God, the closer we come to all our brothers and sisters in the human family. God is not a private God. The God who dwells in our inner sanctuary is also the God who dwells in the inner sanctuary of each human being" (33:22). This place where God and humanity touch one another lies hidden in every human heart. It's not for the taking, just as God himself cannot be taken, let alone understood. If you think that you've captured God, God is already one step ahead of you. This negative theology, saying who or what God is not, is one of the hallmarks of mystical theology.

What I mean to say is that Nouwen's spirituality gradually became more and more mystical. His speaking and writing bore fewer traces of the religious discovery (spirituality) and more of the religious encounter (mysticism).[72] To what extent is one a prerequisite for the other? To what extent can Nouwen be called a mystic? And where do we locate the passage from Christian spirituality to Christian mysticism? I prefer taking a more detached attitude at this point in order to keep the bird from being suspended in mid-air. But as I see it, the Nouwen from before his accident is different from the one after it. Did he see or encounter God? "Now I felt his presence in a most tangible way, as if my whole life had come together and I was being enfolded in love. The homecoming had a real quality of return, a return to the womb of God" (26:37–38). After that, in 1992, he wrote his book on the homecoming of the prodigal son, on his own homecoming, "Here at Daybreak, I have been led to an inner place where I had not been before. It is the place within me where God has chosen to dwell" (29:14). I don't think you could write such a book if you had not been "on the summits" (Hammarskjöld). Here everything stops and at the same time everything comes to life, far beyond the borders of life and death.

"From the heart arise unknowable impulses as well as conscious feelings, moods, and wishes. The heart, too, has its reasons and is the center of perception and understanding. Finally, the heart is the seat of the will: it makes plans and comes to good decisions. Thus the heart is the central and unifying organ of our

personal life. Our heart determines our personality and is therefore not only the place where God dwells but also the place to
which Satan directs his fiercest attacks. It is this heart that is the
place of prayer. The prayer of the heart is a prayer that directs
itself to God from the center of the person and thus affects the
whole of our humanness" (13:77).[73]

– 19 –

SILENCE AROUND THE WORD

Use of the Bible

In the last chapter of this theological section I want to discuss the place that the Bible plays in Nouwen's work and spirituality. To facilitate such a discussion, I undertook a little research and surveyed the use of biblical passages in his books. I begin by covering a few more or less technical features of this research and then go into the content.

What is immediately noticeable is the fact that the First Testament (Tanakh, or the Old Testament) is barely mentioned. Here and there are a few references, among them the "mystical" experience of Elijah in 1 Kings 19. The main exception to this almost total absence of the Tanakh is the use of the Psalms. Many verses from the Psalms and sometimes whole Psalms are quoted.

On this point I might add that Judaism and Jewish spirituality aren't included at all. Among Jewish writers I found Elie Wiesel and Abraham Joshua Heschel cited. I did find in *Cry for Mercy* (15) a prayer which is placed against the background of Jesus' Jewishness. "Dear Lord, you came to this world not only as a human being, but specifically as a Jew. I will never fully understand your words, your gestures, your actions unless I fully realize your Jewishness" (15:60). Whether this marginality of the Jewish tradition gives Nouwen's spirituality a certain unworldliness will be a task for further research. In several places in this book I have demonstrated that this is an area of possible criticism in his work.

Second, Nouwen's writings are filled with quotes from the Gospels. Eight of his books are directly concerned with them. The one that is most frequently quoted, much more than the other three, is the Gospel of John. He also derives most of his spiritual insights from John's Gospel. Nouwen's spirituality is thoroughly Johannine. This most intimate Gospel, so different from the three Synoptics, is clearly his favorite. In the close relationship between the Father and the Son, to which John so emphatically testifies, Nouwen recognizes the relationship between God and humanity, between Jesus and humanity, between God (Jesus) and himself.

Of the many quotes from the Gospel, John 21:18 comes up most often. "Very truly, I tell you, when you were younger, you used to fasten your own belt and to go wherever you wished. But when you grow old, you will stretch out your hands, and someone else will fasten a belt around you and take you where you do not wish to go." I will come back to this text again shortly.

Third, the letters of Paul come up occasionally. There was in Nouwen a partiality for the Christ hymn in Philippians 2, in which kenosis, the self-emptying of Christ is central. We have already noted this text a few times in relation to this discussion. It was the point of departure for the book *Compassion* (16). Passages from Paul in Galatians 2:20 and 1 Thessalonians 5:17 are also striking. In Galatians 2:20 we read: "I have been crucified with Christ; yet I live, no longer I, but Christ lives in me." This is considered the classical text with reference to mysticism and the Bible.[74] In 1 Thessalonians 5:17 is the passage about "praying without ceasing." In *The Way of the Heart* (13), among several similar references, this text from the hesychastic tradition is more fully developed.

Finally, with regard to the other epistles and the Revelation of John, there are quotes from these books spread throughout Nouwen's works, but not in great quantities. Out of this collection the letters of John receive the most attention, prominent among them the passage from 1 John 3:20, which explains that God is greater than our heart.

It can be concluded that Nouwen concentrates on the Psalms and the Gospels. Of the four Gospels, the Gospel of John is the most frequently quoted and the passage from John 18:21 "scores" the highest of all the quoted material. Whether these

biblical selections put Nouwen in the long line of spiritual and
mystical writers is for others to determine.

Meditative Bible Reading

We concluded earlier that Nouwen's approach to theology is quite
special; the same is true of his approach to the Bible. "To take the
holy scriptures and read them is the first thing we have to do to
open ourselves to God's call. Reading the scriptures is not as easy
as it seems since in our academic world we tend to make anything
and everything we read subject to analysis and discussion. But the
word of God should lead us first of all to contemplation and meditation. Instead of taking the words apart, we should bring them
together in our innermost being; instead of wondering if we agree
or disagree, we should wonder which words are directly spoken
to us and connect directly with our most personal story. Instead of
thinking about the words as potential subjects for an interesting
dialogue or paper, we should be willing to let them penetrate into
the most hidden corners of our heart, even to those places where
no other word has yet found entrance. Then and only then can
the word bear fruit as seed sown in rich soil" (8:96–97). I would
like to describe this approach to using the Bible as "meditative
Bible reading." It is very characteristic of writers inclined toward
mysticism, and is completely consistent with Nouwen's preferred
approach to theology.[75]

Is it going too far to say that many discussions in church circles and among believers get bogged down whenever the Bible is
brought up? The Protestant churches in particular are often split
on questions such as scriptural authority and the use of scripture. The question of truth, the question of whether events in the
Bible really happened or not, still preoccupies many hearts. For
people who read the Bible meditatively (or contemplatively), these
questions are no longer of importance. For them it is important
that the texts, and especially the stories, bring Christ closer, that
the texts enlighten their personal lives with Christ. In this way
the texts and the stories become mirrors to guide our lives, and

through a growing familiarity with the texts things are added to our lives. Things? No, we learn to discover that God plays a role in our lives, an all-determining role, for the salvation and healing of ourselves and the world.

It is important to point out that Nouwen did not want to skirt the questions of biblical scholarship, but the exegetical scholarly approach was not his first priority. The presupposition therefore is that the Eternal One is somehow involved in the texts and stories that are "about" him. The words of scripture are in this sense not just words, but words with eternal value. By showing us how this meditative reading works, Nouwen avoids imbuing the words of the Bible with the burdensome dogmatic cargo we know so well from the (ultra)orthodox and fundamentalist circles. Nouwen's book *The Return of the Prodigal Son* (29), based on Luke 15, can be regarded as the most successful attempt of this use of the Bible. The here and now of our times, the individual paths that people take, the penetrating assistance of the artist (Rembrandt) — it is all meditatively read into the story, while the dynamics of the story itself in fact determine the direction. "Reading in a spiritual way is reading with a desire to let God come closer to us.... The purpose of spiritual reading, however, is not to master knowledge or information, but to let God's Spirit master us. Strange as it may sound, spiritual reading means to let ourselves be read by God!" (33:72).[76]

The Bible and Silence

If there's something that occupies writers and poets of the spiritual life, it is certainly the effect of silence. Time and time again they stress that silence is the space where the mysteries between God and humanity have a chance of coming to light. At the same time they are also nearly unanimous in their opinion that it is extremely difficult to enter into this quiet space, and that we as human beings therefore are inclined to quickly run away from silence and to fill it with noise, chaos, and boisterousness. You have to really force yourself to be quiet — it is a spiritual discipline. "Silence is the discipline that helps us to go beyond the entertainment quality of our lives" (35:94). When during his stay in the Trappist monastery Nouwen had to leave the abbey for a visit elsewhere, he wrote upon returning, "With the diminishing silence, a sense of inner contamination developed. In the beginning, I didn't know why I felt somewhat dirty, dusty, impure, but it dawned on me that the lack of silence might have been the main cause" (9:113). When we are completely taken up in the hectic activity of our everyday, unsilenced lives, then this has immediate ethical consequences. Without silence there is scarcely room for the other, no matter how actively we are occupied with the other. "Moments of true compassion will remain engraved on our hearts as long as we live. Often these are moments without words: moments of deep silence" (33:106).

It is especially the relationship of the word (and the Word) and silence in which Nouwen creates a tense dialetic between the two concepts. "Contemplative reading of the holy scriptures and silent time in the presence of God belong closely together. The word of God draws us into silence; silence makes us attentive to God's word. The word of God penetrates through the thick of human verbosity to the silent center of our heart; silence opens in us the space where the word can be heard. Without reading the word, silence becomes stale, and without silence, the word loses its recreative power. The word leads to silence and silence to the word. The word is born in silence, and silence is the deepest response to the word" (8:97).

This is the mutually adjusting activity of word and silence with which Nouwen on the one hand hopes to avoid a sterile verbal theology and on the other hopes to call a halt to a lightheaded spiritualism. I consider this an extremely valuable approach, even from an ecumenical perspective, because the Reformation leans toward the one (the Word) and Catholicism toward the other (silence, ritual, and symbolism). No, says Nouwen, "Silence without speaking is as dangerous as solitude without community" (35:96–97). But just as dangerous is speaking that does not find its roots in silence, and that applies to speaking and writing among people themselves, often "small talk" that has no purpose and only fills up time uselessly. But this dialectic is also essential for God and for talking about God. God is not completely contained in the Word (the Bible) and the Word does not say everything about God. I often say, if it is true that God is greater than the human heart (1 John 3:20) then God is certainly greater than the words that human beings — no matter how inspired they may be — have spoken about the Eternal One. And yet we have to make do with the Word that lies before us, that Word that through the centuries has brought people to God and God to people.

There is a distance between God and the Word, but there is also a close proximity. The space between God and the Word has its source in the silence of God. Nouwen raises the tension to greater heights whenever he tries to describe this dialectic. "Here we can glimpse the great mystery in which we participate through silence and the Word, the mystery of God's own speaking. Out of his eternal silence God spoke the Word, and through this Word created and recreated the world. In the beginning God spoke the land, the sea, and the sky. He spoke the sun, the moon, and the stars. He spoke plants, birds, fish, animals wild and tame. Finally, he spoke man and woman. Then, in the fullness of time, God's Word, through whom all had been created, became flesh and gave power to all who believe to become the children of God. In all this, the Word of God does not break the silence of God, but rather unfolds the immeasurable richness of his silence" (13:56–57).[77] Language possesses a tension that cannot prove the Real One, for the Real One cannot be captured in words. And yet, that which fills the heart also pours out of the mouth.[78]

Part 5

AND TAKE YOU WHERE YOU DO NOT WISH TO GO . . .

– 20 –

SOMEONE ELSE WILL FASTEN
A BELT AROUND YOU

"Very truly, I tell you, when you were younger, you used to fasten your own belt and to go wherever you wished. But when you grow old, you will stretch out your hands, and someone else will fasten a belt around you and take you where you do not wish to go" (John 21:18). This text is a major theme in the works of Henri Nouwen, often explicitly quoted and sometimes implicit in the words and sentences.[79] It is a leitmotif, experienced by Nouwen as the deepest kind of human wisdom: daring to release the grip on one's own life, admitting that you are not the boss of your life, but that Another is close to you, deep inside you, wanting to lead your life into green pastures. The whole of John's Gospel culminates in this "profession of faith." All of the stories about Jesus are so many learning moments for becoming mature and growing spiritually toward these new vistas. But, Nouwen warns, don't wait for that ultimate moment; let the words grow in you now, now is the time to try to drink them all in.

It is just that willingness to try that means you are actively working on your spiritual life and spiritual growth and has positive consequences for your environment. "Here we can see that a growing surrender to the unknown is a sign of spiritual maturity and does not take away autonomy.... I am constantly struck by the fact that those who are most detached from life, those who have learned through living that there is nothing and nobody in this life to cling to, are the really creative people. They are free to move constantly away from the familiar, safe places and can keep moving forward to new, unexplored areas of life" (17:52).

Expanding horizons, indeed. Nouwen himself spent some time in a monastery and in Latin America. He went from Harvard to L'Arche. He wrote about this last move in the context of John 21:18: "The move from Harvard to L'Arche proved to be but one little step from bystander to participant, from judge to repentant sinner, from teacher about love to being loved as the beloved. I really did not have an inkling of how difficult the journey would be. I did not realize how deeply rooted my resistance was and how agonizing it would be to 'come to my senses,' fall on my knees, and let my tears flow freely. I did not realize how hard it would be to become truly part of the great event that Rembrandt's painting portrays. Each little step toward the center seemed like an impossible demand, a demand requiring me to let go one more time from wanting to be in control, to give up one more time the desire to predict life, to die one more time to the fear of not knowing where it all will lead, and to surrender one more time to a love that knows no limits" (29:12–13).

Each person's life is summed up in the short, succinct sentences from the Gospel of John, and the essence of Jesus' own life is summed up there as well. This is what we must learn, step by step, with a lot of falling and getting up again. John places the words of that moving dialogue between Jesus and Peter after the resurrection, for only then do the scales fall from our eyes, just as only after the resurrection do the travelers to Emmaus recognize him in the breaking of the bread. Only then, when we have experienced suffering and death or have anxiously seen it in others and in the world around us — only then do these words of Jesus burn within us. We see that these verses from John become condensed in Nouwen over the years. The component of human suffering is given more room. No one can escape suffering, and this causes anxiety and despair, which already may hang around our necks like dreaded ropes, ready to choke us.

Nouwen does not solve the very difficult theme regarding the reason for human suffering, but with full confidence he abandons himself to hope. Once again, in reference to this text, Nouwen explains, "We, too, must move from action to 'passion,' from being in control to being dependent, from taking initiatives to having to wait, from living to dying. Painful and nearly impossible as this move seems to be, it is in this movement that our true fruitfulness is hidden. Our years of action are years of success and accomplishment. During these years, we do things about which we can speak with pride. But much of this success and many of these accomplishments will soon lie behind us. We might still point to them in the form of trophies, medals, or artistic products. But what is beyond our success and productivity? Fruitfulness lies beyond and that fruitfulness comes through passion, or suffering. Just as the ground can only bear fruit if broken by the plow, our own lives can only be fruitful if opened through passion. Suffering is precisely 'undergoing' action by others, over which we have no control. Dying is always suffering, because dying always puts us in the place where others do to us whatever they decide to do, good or bad" (31:92–93).

– 21 –

A RESTLESS SEEKING
FOR GOD

The subtitle of this book is *A Restless Seeking for God*. In these five words we can sum up the life of Henri Nouwen. But my intention was not only to elucidate and magnify his life in the pages of this book. It is my hope that in the themes that Nouwen touches on and that I have mapped out here all our own searches are made visible. The spiritual life, and certainly writing about it, is not an exclusive pursuit. That's not the way Nouwen wrote about it; his spirituality is inclusive. Is it not often the lives of others who cross our paths and touch our life journeys that enable us to search further ourselves? Our human search for truth, justice, and eternity, if it is a good one, always carries within itself a certain amount of restlessness. What exists, what we see before our eyes, is still very incomplete. We ourselves are not yet where we ought to be. Spirituality and restlessness — there is a link between them both. Our existence is filled with an immense longing. It is a longing that is always eager to be aroused because of the danger of it falling into an easygoing calmness. Restlessly we search further.

Those who heard Henri Nouwen or saw him in action, those who may have followed him or accompanied him, were affected by his restlessness. His arms and legs were fully engaged when he spoke to a room full of people. And in the heat of the argument his whole body danced around the podium. The depth of his words was relieved by the agility of his humor. If the discussion became too "heavy," he would reach for a song from Taizé,

"Let's especially be singing people!" Nouwen was a true "entertainer"; he kept people interested in God, in Jesus. We called that his "clowning spirituality," simple and contagious, never difficult and often consoling. His listeners and readers were "given a wide berth," pulled out of the oppressiveness of their daily occupations.

You had to keep a close watch on his hands; they backed up his words like exclamation or question marks. You could notice in his line of reasoning that not everything could be put into words, that we had to be able to go beyond words, that there is a fire burning in each human life. But don't give up the search, he explained, don't get stuck, stretch out your hands, dare to be led, don't be afraid. A restless seeking for God. For the Eternal One is a fire that burns to warm every human being, a well that rises up in humanity and society. The truth must come out — and it does every now and then, in a lecture, a book, a sermon. God is not a formula, and certainly not a theological formula. You cannot reason out the Eternal One like some known quantity, nor can you regard God as an object of human investigation. For Nouwen God is rather Someone, hidden but nevertheless present in our lives and the life of this world, as a living reality, most brilliantly illuminated in humanity. Jesus is his name, "and our heart is restless, until it rests in You." Augustine committed these intimate words to his journal back in the fourth century.

Every time I read the books of Henri Nouwen I can see him dancing on the stage, I can see his hands breaking and sharing bread in the midst of the vulnerable people of Daybreak, I can see his arms around Adam's broken body, I can see him with me during a pleasant dinner. Henri Nouwen, an unbelievably restless man, yet a man who gradually felt more at home in the safe place within himself. Henri Nouwen, an eternal seeker, but someone who in the midst of all that searching gradually realized that he was being found. Searching for God, but gradually discovering that God was even more intensely searching for him, as his beloved. Henri Nouwen, a man like you and me. All people, women, men, and children, on a persistent search for wholeness in themselves and this world, until God is all in all.

AFTERWORD

My own search through the work of Henri Nouwen is at an end, at least for the time being, because I understand that there are a number of new works on the way which may already have been published by the time this book appears. More than once I have insisted that his work is not yet "over," just as his life is not yet really "over." There was so much left to say, so much that was waiting for reflection. I had hoped that in the coming years, after he had removed himself somewhat from active "service," Nouwen would have been be able to find the rest and room to carry out this more intense work. I'll mention a few possible "projects" that I had thought might be in line with his development.

I had hoped that Nouwen would be able to write a few more books like *The Return of the Prodigal Son* (29). His readers were anxiously awaiting them. And I was looking forward to his "circus book" with great anticipation.[80]

I believe that Nouwen could have helped his readers in an extraordinary way by reflecting on and writing about physicality, a wide open field, and a very new one for theology. I raised this question on pages 69 and 150. What can be said about the body from a spiritual point of view? This could have been directly linked to Nouwen's interest in people suffering from AIDS. Here and there he mentioned this wasting disease and reported the number of his friends who had died of AIDS. What is new about AIDS, especially in the spiritual sense?

The churches and the church are both almost absent themes in Nouwen's work. It might have been interesting if he had ventured a kind of "spiritual ecclesiology" — his own study of the church. Is silence about certain situations and abuses in the church not highly unspiritual? That women have been made second-class members, that homosexuals are still regarded with disgust, were these situations outside his purview?

In the Nouwen archives at Yale, I reviewed a broad and ambitious study (written in Dutch around 1960) about homosexuality. This paper is certainly dated, but a reworking and adaptation might have provided excellent insights. Doesn't the theology of homosexuality deserve a spiritual Christian interpretation? Nouwen had always wanted to write a book about Vincent Van Gogh. In his archives are hundreds of pages of notes made during his classes and seminars. "Few writers or painters have influenced me as much as Vincent. This deeply wounded and immensely gifted Dutchman brought me in touch with my own brokenness and talents in ways nobody else could."[81] Many people were eagerly awaiting a book by Nouwen on Van Gogh. Faith and spirituality are not only about the word but also about the image, "the picture." Today's television culture has made people more image-oriented. In his strikingly beautiful paintings it was *faith* that Van Gogh was portraying.

Eye to Eye

I have not disguised my admiration for the person and the work of Henri Nouwen. The criticisms that I have voiced here and there cannot and should not be left out of a book like this, but they by no means stand in the way of my admiration. On the contrary, I would say. I hope that I have been able to fulfill the hope I expressed in the preface, and that the portrait that I have painted here of Henri Nouwen has lived up to its promise. I have not hidden myself behind him, but in this book we stand eye to eye. "The true biographer, that is to say the one who really wants to know what he can discover behind the mask, enters into a confrontation with himself via his subject. The author who unravels the secrets of an entire human life thereby places great value on his own secrets. As long as he does not push his main subject aside, the best and most fascinating biography is at the same time the creed of the biographer."[82]

Henri with his father, L. J. M. Nouwen, Geysteren, 1993.

As pastor at Daybreak. Celebrating Easter in the chapel, 1996.

IN MEMORIAM: HENRI NOUWEN

At the beginning of September 1996 I spoke with Henri by telephone. We discussed plans to organize a festive presentation for the publication of this book. The plans began shaping up: one evening in Amsterdam and another evening in Antwerp. Henri would be there; the dates were set for January 1997 and the halls were reserved. Henri: "It would be great if we could meet one another on Wednesday, September 25; you can pick me up at Amsterdam airport so we can quietly continue our discussion." Henri would be off on another long trip. He would be traveling to Saint Petersburg with the television team of Jan van den Bosch to do some filming about his book *The Return of the Prodigal Son*. After all, Rembrandt's famous painting of the prodigal son is hanging there in the Hermitage. From Tuesday the 17th until Tuesday the 24th of September he would be staying in Saint Petersburg with the television crew. "Is this something you really want to do?" I asked him. "It is quite an undertaking." He answered, "Yes and no. The film is a good idea, but it's so exhausting and I'm already so tired." "So tired" — something I heard him say with more and more frequency.

So it was good that after ten years of hard work at Daybreak he had just enjoyed another long sabbatical period from September 1995 to September 1996. But it was not a real sabbatical — not a year of rest. It's true that he had spent it away from Daybreak, but he still spent it "flying" all over the place. It seemed as though he was trying to write several books in one last burst of energy. An unconscious fight against the clock? He wrote books 35, 37,

A photo taken during the reception of an honorary doctorate at Maryknoll, New York. From left to right: Henri, Jurjen Beumer (the author), Carl Macmillan, Bill van Buren, May 1995.

Summer 1996.
One of the last pictures
of Henri Nouwen.

and 38 during this sabbatical period (see the bibliography), and a number of others stood in line.

It was striking (and it certainly is in retrospect) that he spent more time than ever in the country of his birth, the Netherlands — with his father, with whom he spent a week on vacation in the Ardennes in July, with the rest of his family, and with us, his friends. It was good to hear that he would be giving up his pastoral responsibilities at Daybreak and would get a successor. His living quarters, above the small community chapel, would be expanded into a little house. And construction on Dayspring, the new chapel, would begin very soon. It would have to be a good spot for daily worship as well as a location for retreats and for receiving guests from outside the community. Henri worked hard to realize these plans. This kind of place for prayer had been his longtime dream.

So a new and final phase in Henri Nouwen's life was being planned and charted. From this quiet place he would be able to maintain his numerous contacts and continue to travel. Sunday evening, September 15, 1996, his plane left Toronto for Amsterdam. He was taken from Schiphol airport to a hotel in Hilversum. Just one day of rest and preparation and then the journey would continue to Saint Petersburg on Wednesday. He became ill in his hotel room; it was his heart. He was taken immediately to the hospital. Critical hours followed. Would he survive? His immediate family kept watch at his side. Tuesday and Wednesday passed slowly and anxiously. Nathan Ball, director of Daybreak and friend of Henri, arrived from Toronto to be with him. He seemed to be out of danger. Thursday there was some improvement, and by Friday Henri seemed on the way to recovery and began again with his normal hectic pace. The doctor advised him to get out of bed and walk around. He accompanied his friends to the door of the hospital. The closing words of Psalm 91 still resounded as Henri prepared for the night that Friday.

> The night will never overcome him
> his days will stand forever.

Though thousands may fall dead
    he will always be inscribed
    in the palm of God's hand.
God protects those who trust,
    who live out of faith alone.
God will build a new heaven
    out of the love
    which flows from their tears.

The following day, Saturday September 21, 1996, was Henri Nouwen's last day of life. What no one had expected happened; a second major heart attack occurred and was fatal. He died in the early hours of the morning, alone. The consternation and sorrow were immense. His father, ninety-three years old, prayed the Our Father at the bed of his dead son. An unfathomable feeling of loss was slowly overcoming everyone. At Daybreak the community was in tears. The handicapped members were completely grief-stricken. How would the assistants be able to console them as well as themselves?

Sue Mosteller, Joe Egan, Lorenzo, and Gordi flew from Toronto to Amsterdam. Henri was laid out in a funeral home in Hilversum. Tuesday afternoon there was a wake for his family and close friends, an afternoon of quiet and prayer beside Henri's body. On Wednesday morning, September 25, in the same cathedral during a eucharistic celebration, farewell was said to Henri Nouwen. The church was completely filled with family, friends, and acquaintances. Henri's archbishop, Adrianus Cardinal Simonis, was the celebrant. Jean Vanier, the founder of the L'Arche movement, gave a very penetrating meditation. The casket was surrounded by sunflowers, flowers that always turn toward the sun, toward the light. It was as if the great painter of sunflowers, Vincent Van Gogh, was winking at his friend Henri Nouwen who had written and thought about him so much.

The farewell, *adieu* ("go to God"), was given by Henri's brother Paul. "We wanted so much to hold on to you and bury you in Geysteren, in the restfulness of the forests and the rippling of the River Maas, so close to father. But father and all of us

The funeral Mass in Utrecht, September 25, 1996
(photo by Werry Crone).

The simple wooden cross on
Henri's grave, Sacred Heart
Cemetery, Toronto, Canada.

believe that we must let you go once again, just as we did forty
years ago. You're off on another journey, but now to your well-
earned resting place. And that is Daybreak in Ontario. We want to
cross the bridge between our family and your family at Daybreak.
We want to build a long bridge over the ocean between Europe and
Canada. We want to accompany you this Thursday to Toronto, to
Richmond Hill, to Daybreak, and let you rest among your own,
among your family where you finally have found your home."

On Thursday, September 26, the embalmed body of Henri Nouwen was flown to Toronto. His father, both his brothers, and his
sister accompanied him. Daybreak mourned around the body that
lay in honor in the gathering room of the community. The next
day Henri's body was carried to the parish church a little distance
away, where Henri regularly celebrated the Eucharist and gave
homilies. People came to the funeral from all over the U.S. and
Canada. Professors stood next to the handicapped, the young next
to the old, Catholics next to Protestants, Jews, and nonbelievers.
The family carried the chalice that Henri had received from his
Uncle Toon at his ordination with the mandate to "take it, but pass
it on to the next member of our family to be ordained" (35:16–
17). They handed it over to Daybreak, acknowledging them as the
next in the family "ordained" to carry the chalice onward.

During the afternoon of Saturday, September 28, 1996, Henri
Nouwen was buried in a quiet corner of the little Sacred Heart
Cemetery near Toronto. A simple wooden cross with his name
and dates (24 January 1932–21 September 1996) marks the spot.
On the day of his burial another new book appeared from Henri's
hand, *The Inner Voice of Love: A Journey through Anguish to
Freedom.* It closes with these words: "During my months of anguish, I often wondered if God is real or just a product of my
imagination. I now know that while I felt completely abandoned,
God didn't leave me alone. Many friends and family members
have died during the past eight years, and my own death is not
so far away. But I have heard the inner voice of love, deeper and
stronger than ever. I want to keep trusting in that voice and be
led by it beyond the boundaries of my short life, to where God is
all in all" (37:118).

NOTES

1. An autobiography summarizing this entire life is Laurent J. M. Nouwen, *Mijn laaste biecht: Kritische reflecties van een oud man aan het einde van zijn carrière als schrijver en fiscalist* (My last confession: critical reflections of an old man at the end of his career as writer and lawyer; Baarn: Tielt, 1995).

2. In a highly personal way, the father tells the story of his son in a small booklet, Laurent J. M. Nouwen: *Henri's vader vertelt: Zo maar een verhaal over een doorsnee-katholiek gezin uit de eerste helft van deze eeuw waarvan de eerstgeboren zoon bereids in zijn prille jeugd blijk gaf van zijn passie voor het priesterschap* (Henri's father speaks: just the story of an average Catholic family from the first half of this century whose first-born son showed signs of a passion for the priesthood, even in his tenderest years; privately printed and distributed within a small circle).

3. T. H. M. van Schaik, *Vertrouwde Vreemden: Betrekkingen tussen katholieken en joden in Nederland 1930–1990* (Familiar strangers: the relationship between Catholics and Jews in the Netherlands 1930–1990; Baarn, 1992), 55. Because of the important role of Ramselaar, a short biography of him is given in this book, 54ff. Right after his priestly ordination he went to study music in Rome. Van Schaik writes about "Ramselaar's alleged partly-Jewish origin" (56) and marks him as "a man of the world: an amiable presence with a broad interest in culture, artistically gifted, blessed with a fine perception of 'what was brewing,' courteous and considerate in his relationship with women and a man of means to boot" (57). Henri was very fond of this uncle. The supposed Jewish roots of this uncle Toon Ramselaar (and thus also of Henri Nouwen's mother) are not based on truth, according to the family.

4. I have come across the name of Han Fortmann only in Nouwen's book *Aging* (1974) because of his words on his deathbed (6).

5. He recalled his time in the army many years later when he was in the hospital following a serious accident (see chapter 14). His life was in danger. When the situation grew more serious, he wanted to tell his colleague Sue Mosteller and all whom he had offended that he was asking their forgiveness. He wrote then: "As I said this, I felt I was taking off the wide leather belts that I had worn while chaplain with the rank of captain in the army. Those belts not only girded my waist, but also crossed over my chest and shoulders. They had given me prestige and power. They had encouraged me to judge people and put them in their place. Although my stay in the army was very brief, I had, in my mind, never fully removed these belts. But I knew now that I did not want to die with

these belts holding me captive. I had to die powerless, without belts, completely free from judgment" (26:41–42).

6. In *The Wounded Healer* (1972) he used images from this time to describe the "professional loneliness" of the minister. "There was a time, not too long ago, when we felt like captains running our own ships — with a great sense of power and self-confidence. Now we are standing in the way. That is our lonely position. We are powerless, on the side, liked maybe by a few crew members who swab the decks and goof off to drink a beer with us, but not taken very seriously when the weather is fine. The wound of our loneliness is indeed deep" (5:86–87).

7. Nouwen dedicated his book *Creative Ministry* (1971) to Seward Hiltner, "teacher and friend, who introduced me into the field of pastoral theology." In a book written later, *The Living Reminder* (10), he worked out the themes of Hiltner's book *Preface to Pastoral Theology* in a spiritual direction.

8. H. Faber, W. J. Berger, and W. Zijlstra introduced the concept of Clinical Pastoral Education into the Netherlands. See W. Zijlstra, *Klinische Pastorale Vorming* (Nijmegen, 1973). On the development of this, see T. Kruyne, "Geschiedenis van de Klinische Pastorale Vorming in Nederland," in *Ontginningswerk, bijdragen voor dr. Wybe Zijlstra* (Kampen, 1985).

9. Henri Nouwen, "De mars van Selma naar Montgomery" (The march from Selma to Montgomery), in *Sjaloom,* October 1965.

10. Visiting professor in the Department of Psychology at the University of Notre Dame in Indiana. Taught Clinical Psychology, Developmental Psychology, Personality Theory, Psychology of Religion, Pastoral Psychology.

11. "This book is the result of a two-year 'visit' to the University of Notre Dame" (1:vii).

12. In series III of the Henri J. M. Nouwen Papers, Archives and Manuscripts Group Number 68 (revised April 1994), 6, in which the archives of Nouwen are described (preserved by Yale University), we can peruse Nouwen's lecture notes and other unpublished materials dealing with these three people. Boisen: "At the beginning of Clinical Pastoral Training stands one man: Anton Theophilus Boisen (1876–1965). A man with genial traits, who, thanks to his extraordinary gifts and thanks to his illness (he suffered attacks of degeneracy psychosis), laid the groundwork for a movement that now covers all of America." So begins W. Zijlstra's book *Klinische Pastorale Vorming* (Nijmegen, 1973); and he follows with a few pages of a short biography of this outstanding man. In the same book by Zijlstra, Seward Hiltner is also mentioned as one "who as a writer, teacher, and organizer had done exceptional work for CPT" (4). Later Hiltner would adapt the insights of the psychologist Carl Rogers (see his work *Client Centered Therapy,* 1951) for ministry. Under the heading "relationship between psychosis and conversion" Han Fortmann also speaks about Anton Boisen. "So it is understandable that Boisen did not want to see religion as an attempt to escape hard reality, as Freud and Marx did, but rather as an active attempt to gain answers to the last questions" (*Als ziende de onzienlijke (II)* [On seeing the Invisible; Hilversum, 1974], 393). Hiltner: In a letter to Annet van Lindenberg, dated February 2, 1988 (included in her master's thesis "Weest stil, en

weet..., De betekenis van het werk van Henri J. M. Nouwen voor de praktijk van het protestantse pastoraat" (Be still, and know...The meaning of the work of Henri J. M. Nouwen for the practice of Protestant ministry; TU Kampen, 1988, unpublished). Nouwen wrote that the influence of Hiltner on him was "mainly that of a guide." And further on: "I have studied all of his work and I have made many of his ideas my own, but I am steadily more convinced of the necessity of a pastoral approach that is strongly influenced by the spiritual life of the pastor." Nouwen developed this "method" in his book *Creative Ministry* (1972), and he dedicated this book to Seward Hiltner. The themes of Nouwen's later book *The Living Reminder* (10), such as healing, sustaining, and guiding, are borrowed from Hiltner "in order to express how much thanks I have for my teacher Seward Hiltner" (14).

13. "I met him once, on the grounds of the Abbey of Gethsemani in Kentucky. Since then his person and work have had so much influence on me that his sudden death hit me like the death of one of my best friends" (2:7). In the same letter to Annet van Lindenberg (see note 12) he wrote that Merton also had a great influence on him "but probably more through his personality than through what he wrote."

14. Associate professor in Pastoral Theology at Yale Divinity School, New Haven, Connecticut. Taught (1) Courses on Ministry: General Introductory Course. Discipline and Discipleship, Ministry to the Elderly, Ministry to Prisoners, Ministry in Non-Religious Institutions, Ministry as Hospitality, The Ministry of Vincent van Gogh, and (2) Courses on Spirituality: General Course on the Relationship between Ministry and Spirituality, The History of Christian Spirituality, The Life and Works of Thomas Merton, On Prayer. Received tenure in 1974. Made full professor in Pastoral Theology in 1977. Taught at Yale Divinity School until June 1981.

15. "The Council was overtaken by the many new ideas that had developed in society before the Catholic Church had the time to properly assimilate all the liberal achievements. This put the Council under criticism from both right and left." E. Schillebeeckx, *Theologisch testament: Notarieel nog niet verleden* ((Theological testament; Baarn, 1994), 42.

16. During his years in the Netherlands, Nouwen did travel to Cuernavaca in Mexico, where he got to know Ivan Illich, and to Los Angeles, California, where he met Mario Savio and through his friend Richard White he came into direct contact with the student revolution. Later Nouwen wrote a biography about Richard White, "Man at the Watershed," a book that White found too dangerous to publish at the time. It has never been published.

17. And when he did try to penetrate this world for a good friend (Fred), he was not understood. See the honest account of this in the afterword of *Life of the Beloved* (28). "Fred: 'Although you express to us what is most precious to you, you do not realize how far we are from where you are. You speak from a context and tradition that is alien to us.'...Fred said many other things, but the main response to all I had written was that I had not truly entered into the secular mentality" (28:115–16).

18. The other two journals are *Gracias* (18) and *The Road to Daybreak* (23).

19. This quote is more instinctive on his part than factually correct, because the book *Reaching Out* (8) demonstrates a strong unity of thought and feelings.

20. G. Gutiérrez's *A Theology of Liberation* came out in 1973, and the fruits of this were clearly seen by Nouwen.

21. Ibid., see 152ff.

22. *We Drink From Our Own Wells: The Spiritual Journey of a People* (Maryknoll, N.Y.: Orbis Books, 1984). The introductory preface first appeared in the magazine *America* on October 15, 1983. It is interesting that in the Dutch edition of this book the foreword by Nouwen is left out. In a later book from Gutiérrez about Job the mystical tone is even stronger. "In *On Job: God-Talk and the Suffering of the Innocent* (Maryknoll, N.Y. Orbis Books, 1987) he shows what the deepest mystical foundation of liberation theology is. Unlike what is commonly thought and unlike what the writings of liberation theology sometimes lead one to believe, the focus is not on action or ethics. It is not concerned with calling forth the hidden God, with using hard work or logical revolutionary practices to establish God's kingdom. Naturally, where lives can be saved or suffering relieved, then action is required. But in the final analysis Gutiérrez sees the figure of Job in terms of the spiritual path" (E. Borgman, *Alexamenos aanbidt zijn God: Theologische essays voor sceptische lezers* [Alexamenos prays to his God: theological essays for skeptical readers; Zoetermeer, 1994], 111). And see also the extensive biography by R. McAfee Brown, *Gustavo Gutiérrez: An Introduction to Liberation Theology* (Maryknoll, N.Y.: Orbis Books, 1990).

23. Prayer, life with the poor, and life in community — these three are the veins and arteries of Nouwen's spirituality. In Genesee he learned to experience a deep prayer life, in Latin America he learned that contact with the poor is essential for prayer. In Peru he wanted to attain the third major point, a life in community with and among the poor. But he was not able to realize this until Daybreak in the L'Arche movement, the next great phase of his life.

24. Preface to 1993 edition, Maryknoll, N.Y., Orbis Books.

25. Nouwen's foreword to G. Gutiérrez, *We Drink from Our Own Wells* (see note 22). My critical question is whether Nouwen ever tried to remedy this weak point in his spirituality, or whether he did not fall back into what he called a "romanticized spirituality" in the years that followed.

26. "In the fall of 1983 I came for the first time to Trosly, France, to visit L'Arche, a community for people with mental handicaps, founded by the Canadian Jean Vanier" (21:9).

27. On Jean Vanier, see Kathryn Spink, *Jean Vanier and L'Arche: A Communion of Love* (London, 1990). On the mother of Jean Vanier, see D. and G. Cowley, *One Woman's Journey: A Portrait of Pauline Vanier* (Ottawa, 1993).

28. Henri J. M. Nouwen, "De verborgen schat" (The hidden treasure), in Jurjen Beumer, ed., *Als de hemel de aarde raakt, Spiritualiteit en mystiek, Ervaringen* (When heaven and earth touch: spirituality and mysticism, experiences; Kampen, 1989).

29. Henri J. M. Nouwen, "The Gulf between East and West," in *New Ox-*

ford Review (May 1994): 16. Also "Pilgrimage to the Christian East," *New Oxford Review* (April 1994).

30. The difficulty of a real and balanced friendship is described concretely at the end of *The Road to Daybreak* (23), in which a friend (Nathan) can supplant "the first love" and commitment to the community (23:223).

31. Henri J. M. Nouwen, "Circus Diary I, Finding the Trapeze Artist in the Priest," *New Oxford Review* (June 1993). Also "Circus Diary II, Finding a New Way to Get a Glimpse of God," *New Oxford Review* (July/August 1993).

32. Henri J. M. Nouwen, "Our Story, Our Wisdom," in *HIV/AIDS: The Second Decade,* a publication of the National Catholic AIDS Network (San Francisco, 1995).

33. This chapter in *Clowning in Rome* is about celibacy.

34. On the day of Nouwen's burial the book was published in which he gives an account of this inner struggle, *The Inner Voice of Love: A Journey through Anguish to Freedom* (37). "I could easily have become bitter, resentful, depressed, and suicidal. That this did not happen was the result of the struggle expressed in this book" (xvii). During this period (December 1987–June 1988) he wrote his so-called "spiritual imperatives" based on the contact with his spiritual directors. These are thoughts that he more or less forces invitingly on himself (and thus on his readers as well).

35. Further along in the text God is also called "Mother."

36. The difference between joy and happiness (pleasure) is explained in *Here and Now* (33:25ff).

37. To say what something is *not,* a proven method in mystical theology, is the so-called "theologia negativa."

38. In this book he describes the way from hostility to hospitality (the level of human relationship), the way from illusion to prayer (the relationship with God), and the way from loneliness to solitude (the personal level). These are "different poles between which our lives vacillate and are held in tension" (10).

39. During the months in the monastery Nouwen learned from John Eudes "that the measure in which we are alone, is the measure in which we can be together with others" (9:47).

40. In *Reaching Out* (8) he speaks on p. 97 about a "guide" or "spiritual director."

41. During the deep crisis in his first year at Daybreak, Nouwen spoke about a "second loneliness." He became entangled in a relationship that was too emotional. The distance that he had to take from it caused this "second loneliness." It is "a loneliness with Jesus in community. I discovered that this second loneliness was much, much harder to live than the loneliness resulting from physical or emotional isolation" (*The Road to Daybreak,* 23:223).

42. The brochure: "DAYSPRING, solitude/community/ministry at L'Arche Daybreak."

43. *De ware verhalen van een Russische pelgrim,* Haarlem, 1977; *The Way of a Pilgrim* (New York: Seabury Press, 1965).

44. Elsewhere he gives some other practical tips: " . . . each day to listen for a half-hour to the voice of love . . . " (28:59), referring to the book from the Hindu

teacher Eknath Easwaran, *Meditation: An Eight-Point Program* (Petaluma, Calif.: Nilgiri Press, 1978). There are also practical tips on prayer in *Here and Now* (33:88), for example, how certain people can give us further help in prayer. "It is very important that our inner room has pictures on its walls, pictures that allow those who enter our lives to have something to look at that tells them where they are and where they are invited to go" (33:95).

45. See chapter 19 about silence.

46. Nouwen's definition of a mystic is someone whose identity is deeply rooted in the "first love" of God. In chapter 18 I take another look at mysticism in Nouwen's spirituality.

47. Nouwen wrote two prayer books: *A Cry for Mercy: Prayers from the Genesee* (15, written during his second period in the monastery) and *Heart Speaks to Heart: Three Prayers to Jesus* (24, written during the year in Trosly).

48. Henri Nouwen, "De verborgen schat," in Jurjen Beumer, ed., *Als de hemel de aarde raakt* (Kampen, 1989), 126. In *Reaching Out* Nouwen also speaks about three types of relationships: "the relationship between parents and their children, the relationship between teachers and their students, and the relationship between professionals — such as doctors, social workers, psychologists, counselors, nurses, ministers, and priests — and their patients, clients, counselees, and parishioners" (8:55).

49. "De verborgen schat," 131.

50. These are the same Greek words as in 1 John 4:19: *prootos* (first) and *agapaoo* (to love).

51. If we divide up Nouwen's manner of writing into the so-called *munus triplex* (the three-fold ministry of Christ as prophet, priest, and king), than we see that the priestly speech dominates.

52. Psychologically speaking, people might question why this theme of the "first love" is so persistent throughout Nouwen's entire work. Did he feel that he had been neglected or deprived as a child? Is there something in him that is trying to emerge but cannot find its way out? "When I was a small child I kept asking my father and mother: 'Do you love me?' I asked that question so often and so persistently that it became a source of irritation to my parents. Even though they assured me hundreds of times that they loved me I never seemed to be satisfied with their answers and kept on asking the same question. Now, many years later, I realize that I wanted a response that they couldn't give" (33:77–78). It is clear that with the above questions we move in another direction: towards a psychoanalytic description of someone's life journey, as the famous psychologist Erik H. Erikson (1904–94) did in his book on Luther, *Young Man Luther* (1958). See also his *Childhood and Society* (New York, 1963). I do not intend to take this psychoanalytic path in this book about Nouwen, though others may want to accept the challenge at the proper time.

53. "What I have learned is that God's unlimited love often expresses itself through the limited love of God's people" (23:213). "Parents, friends, and teachers, even those who speak to me through the media, are mostly very sincere in their concerns. Their warnings and advice are well intended. In fact, they can be limited, human expressions of an unlimited divine love. But when I forget that

voice of the first unconditional love, then these innocent suggestions can easily start dominating my life and pull me into the 'distant country' (29:37)."

54. The concept "being fruitful" (fecundity) is quite a regular feature of Nouwen's work. See for example *Lifesigns: Intimacy, Fecundity and Ecstasy in Christian Perspective* (20:55–81).

55. Nouwen wrote a foreword to the collection of poems of his sister-in-law: Marina San Giorgio, *Een glimlach kwam voorbij* (A smile passed by; Tielt).

56. Cardinal Joseph Bernardin, *The Gift of Peace: Personal Reflections* (Chicago: Loyola University Press, 1997), 128.

57. Nouwen was already using the concept of "last gift" here in *Aging*. Death is the last gift that people leave for those who follow. We will see later that Nouwen's most mature book on death has the title *Our Greatest Gift* (31).

58. In *The Wounded Healer* (5) pastoral care for the dying is defined as waiting. " 'I will wait for you' goes beyond death and is the deepest expression of the fact that faith and hope may pass but love will remain forever" (5:69). Waiting is a favorite concept for Nouwen. See also Henri J. M. Nouwen, *Out of Solitude: Three Meditations on the Christian Life* (7), especially part 3. And Henri J. M. Nouwen, *The Path of Waiting* (34/1).

59. This little book is completely devoted to this accident and working through it spiritually. It is also published as *The Path of Freedom* in a handy set of short books by Nouwen (34/1).

60. With reference to this overactivism, see also *Creative Ministry* (4), especially chapter 4. Nouwen pointed out three dangers in social involvement: spending much effort on overly concrete tasks, the longing for human power, and the ever-present human pride.

61. Nouwen did write about the church in one of his last books, *Bread for the Journey*, days October 15 to November 8.

62. I tried to place Nouwen's ideas by reading Coos Huijsen's article "De terugkeer van de moraal: De culturele dimensie van de politiek," in *Tijdschrift* of December 1995. "One of the interesting and sometimes irritating aspects of communitarianism or neopersonalism is that it cannot simply be called progressive or conservative, nor does it offer a complete political program. Instead it refers to a certain approach, a methodology in which questions about politics are formulated in a fundamentally different fashion. The essence of this is that the underlying values and norms are indeed addressed, as is the question about human beings and their imposition of meaning" (20).

63. I wrote a short spiritual biography of Dag Hammarskjöld in my *Intimiteit & Solidariteit: Over het evenwicht tussen dogmatiek, mystiek en ethiek* (Intimacy and solidarity: on the balance between dogmatics, mysticism, and ethics; Baarn, 1993), 262–304.

64. Very interesting and still very topical is Nouwen's discussion with the "evangelicals," which was already begun in his first book. Besides the respect he has for them is his reproach that they pass over the hard-won insights of modern times and uncritically embrace the old. "The Pentecostals within the Catholic Church act in a way which does not take into account the major development of the recent renewal in Catholic theology" (1:74).

65. These patterns of thought in Nouwen's work consistently lead to the Eucharist or the Last Supper. In doing so he expresses a rather classical and eucharistic theology. I will not go any further into this, but recommend *With Burning Hearts: A Meditation on the Eucharistic Life* (32).

66. Actually the Christian tradition teaches us to speak with *three* words: Father, Son, and *Spirit*. Nouwen's theology and spirituality are more christological than pneumatological, directed more toward Christ than the Spirit. Only in a few places in his work did he speak explicitly about the Holy Spirit; see 14:48 and 16:105.

67. The books *Creative Ministry, The Wounded Healer,* and *Aging* all reach a christological climax in the last paragraphs.

68. Emptying = kenosis (Greek); see 29:95 where Nouwen's kenotic ethic is discussed.

69. The story of Adam is also included in Robert Durback's Henri Nouwen Reader, *Seeds of Hope* (New York: Bantam Books, 1989), 191–205. See also Henri J. M. Nouwen, "Macht, machteloosheid, kracht: Een theologie van de zwakheid" (Power, powerlessness, strength; a theology of weakness), in *Benedictijns Tijdschrift* 2 (1994): 50–60.

70. Henri J. M. Nouwen, "In Memory of Adam," in *Daybreak Newsbreak* (Spring 1996).

71. Henri J. M. Nouwen, *In Memory of Adam Arnett, Written for All Who Have Known and Loved Adam* (private publication). Nouwen did a more complete story of his life with Adam in *Adam: God's Beloved* (38).

72. On this difference between spirituality and mysticism and what makes Christian mysticism mystical, see my *Intimiteit & Solidariteit,* especially chapter 5.

73. On "the heart" see also *Letters to Marc about Jesus* (22), 3 and 81; see also *The Road to Daybreak* (23), 47ff.

74. For more information on this text see my *Intimiteit & Solidariteit,* 146.

75. Nouwen demonstrated the specificity of the word with "sacramental": "The Word of God is sacramental. That means it is sacred, and as a sacred word it makes present what it indicates" (32:45). It is further explained in the context of the Eucharist in *With Burning Hearts: A Meditation on the Eucharistic Life* (32).

76. On this method of using the Bible see also E. H. Peterson, *Working the Angles: The Shape of Pastoral Integrity* (Grand Rapids: Eerdmans, 1993), and K. Waaijman, "Lezen, overwegen, schouwen" (Reading, considering, witnessing), in *Speling* 1 (1996): 76ff.

77. The English text says correctly "God spoke," which is better translated as "God calls (into being)" following the Hebrew text of Genesis 1, which is about "calling." Martin Buber translates, "Gott *rief* dem Licht: Tag!" [God *calls* the light: Day!], etc. So to "create" is to expressively *call* things (human beings, animals) into being.

78. This penetrating theme of silence and the silence of God is nowhere so prodigiously treated as in the book by the French Jewish scholar André Neher (1914–88), *De ballingschap van het Woord: Van de stilte in de Bijbel tot de*

stilte van Auschwitz (The exile of the Word: from silence in the Bible to the silence of Auschwitz; Baarn: Gooi en Sticht, 1992). Nouwen does not quote from this book, and yet there are parallels between his way of thinking and that of Neher. Neher writes that silence "is clean, restful, and stimulating; it is more eloquent than the word, it strengthens, underlines, and intensifies the word; it is like a counterpoint to the word, and in the interstices of the conversation, in the pauses, the moments of delay, it brings as it were an additional excess of life, an unexpected energy that can lift human beings out of themselves and bring them into an encounter with God — the God that does not allow himself to be reached in the fire or in the strong wind, nor in the spirit, but who reaches human beings in the 'soft Voice of silence' (1 Kings 19:12)" (47).

79. Nouwen's book *With Open Hands* (3) ends with this text. *Creative Ministry* (4) uses this text as a motto for the whole book. Besides the places noted in the text, there is also *Compassion* (16:44), *Gracias* (18:54), *The Road to Daybreak* (23:5/156) and the closing lines of this journal: "It becomes increasingly clear to me that Jesus led me to where I never wanted to go" (228).

80. There are quite a few repetitions in Nouwen's works. "It seems sometimes like a grab-bag, which also occasionally has annoying repetitions. Sometimes he would even be accused of 'hack writing' " (Gunter Schollaert, "Krachtlijnen voor een christelijke spiritualiteit in de geschriften van H. Nouwen" [Lines of force for a Christian spirituality in the writings of H. Nouwen], master's thesis at the Catholic University of Louvain, 1989, 107).

81. Foreword by Henri J. M. Nouwen in Cliff Edwards, *Van Gogh and God: A Creative Spiritual Quest* (Chicago, 1989), p. x. For a discussion of Edwards's book and Van Gogh, see my *Zoektocht: Geloofsboek voor kleinverbruikers* (The Search, a book on faith for modest consumers; Baarn, 1991), 42–52.

82. M. van Soest, "Wat drijft de biograaf?" in J. Anthierens, et al., *Aspecten van de literaire biografie* ("What drives the biographer?" in Aspects of literary biography; Kampen, 1990), 45.

BIBLIOGRAPHY OF HENRI NOUWEN'S ENGLISH WORKS

The English-language editions of Henri Nouwen's books are listed here in chronological order. For information about his other writings the reader is referred to the Nouwen archives at Yale Divinity School. It should be noted that eventually most of his journal and magazine articles (revised or not) reappeared in one of his books.

The following list gives only the first year of publication. Most of the books have subsequently gone through numerous printings and editions. At the time of this writing almost all of the titles are still in print and available.

1. *Intimacy: Essays in Pastoral Psychology.* San Francisco: Harper & Row, 1969.

2. *Thomas Merton: Contemplative Critic.* San Francisco: Harper & Row, 1982. Originally published in Dutch by Ambo, Bilthoven, 1970, under the title *Bidden on het Leven, Het Contemplatief engagement van Thomas Merton.* First English edition by Fides (Notre Dame, Ind., 1972), entitled *Pray to Live.*

3. *With Open Hands.* Notre Dame, Ind.: Ave Maria Press, 1972. Originally published in Dutch by Ambo, Bilthoven, 1971, under the title *Met open handen: Notities over het gebed.*

4. *Creative Ministry.* New York: Doubleday, 1972.

5. *The Wounded Healer: Ministry in Contemporary Society.* New York: Doubleday, 1972.

6. *Aging: The Fulfillment of Life* (with Walter J. Gaffney) New York: Doubleday, 1974.

7. *Out of Solitude: Three Meditations on the Christian Life.* Notre Dame, Ind.: Ave Maria Press, 1974.

8. *Reaching Out: The Three Movements of the Spiritual Life.* New York: Doubleday, 1975

9. *The Genesee Diary: Report from a Trappist Monastery.* New York: Doubleday, 1976.

10. *The Living Reminder: Service and Prayer in Memory of Jesus Christ.* Minneapolis: Seabury Press, 1977.

11. *Clowning in Rome: Reflections on Solitude, Celibacy, Prayer, and Contemplation.* New York: Doubleday, 1979.

12. *In Memoriam.* Notre Dame, Ind.: Ave Maria Press, 1980.

13. *The Way of the Heart.* San Francisco: Harper & Row, 1981.

14. *Making All Things New: An Invitation to the Spiritual Life.* San Francisco: Harper & Row, 1981.

15. *A Cry for Mercy: Prayers from the Genesee.* New York: Doubleday, 1981.

16. *Compassion: A Reflection on the Christian Life.* With Donald P. McNeill and Douglas A. Morrison. New York: Doubleday, 1982.

17. *A Letter of Consolation.* New York: Harper & Row, 1982.

18. *Gracias: A Latin American Journal.* San Francisco: Harper & Row, 1983.

19. *Love in a Fearful Land: A Guatemalan Story.* Notre Dame, Ind.: Ave Maria Press, 1985 (out of print).

20. *Lifesigns: Intimacy, Fecundity and Ecstasy in Christian Perspective.* New York: Doubleday, 1986.

21. *Behold the Beauty of the Lord: Praying with Icons.* Notre Dame, Ind.: Ave Maria Press, 1987.

22. *Letters to Marc about Jesus.* San Francisco: Harper & Row, 1988. Originally published in Dutch by Lannoo, Tielt, 1987, under the title *Brieven aan Marc: Over Jezus en de zin van het leven.*

23. *The Road to Daybreak: A Spiritual Journey.* New York: Doubleday, 1988.

24. *Heart Speaks to Heart: Three Prayers to Jesus.* Notre Dame, Ind.: Ave Maria Press, 1989.

25. *In the Name of Jesus: Reflections on Christian Leadership.* New York: Crossroad, 1989.

26. *Beyond the Mirror: Reflections on Death and Life.* New York: Crossroad, 1990.

27. *Walk with Jesus: Stations of the Cross.* Maryknoll, N.Y.: Orbis Books, 1990.

28. *Life of the Beloved: Spiritual Living in a Secular World.* New York: Crossroad, 1992.

29. *The Return of the Prodigal Son: A Meditation on Fathers, Brothers, and Sons.* New York: Doubleday, 1992.

30. *Jesus and Mary: Finding Our Sacred Center.* Cincinnati: St. Anthony Messenger Press, 1993.

31. *Our Greatest Gift: A Meditation on Dying and Caring.* San Francisco: HarperCollins, 1994.

32. *With Burning Hearts: A Meditation on the Eucharistic Life.* Maryknoll, N.Y.: Orbis Books, 1994.

33. *Here and Now: Living in the Spirit.* New York: Crossroad, 1994.

34/1. *The Path of Waiting.* New York: Crossroad, 1995.

34/2. *The Path of Freedom.* New York: Crossroad, 1995.

34/3. *The Path of Power.* New York: Crossroad, 1995.

34/4. *The Path of Peace.* New York: Crossroad, 1995.

35. *Can You Drink This Cup?* Notre Dame, Ind.: Ave Maria Press, 1996.

36. *Bread for the Journey: A Daybook of Wisdom and Faith.* San Francisco: HarperCollins, 1996.

37. *The Inner Voice of Love: A Journey through Anguish to Freedom.* New York: Doubleday, 1996.

38. *Adam: God's Beloved.* Maryknoll, N.Y.: Orbis Books, 1997.

39. *Sabbatical Journey: The Final Year.* New York: Crossroad, 1997.

Please note: apart from some quotations, books 36 through 39 are not dealt with in this biography.

Henri Nouwen's collected works are now being published by Continuum in New York. To date three volumes have been issued under the name Dayspring Edition. Part 1 of the collected works is a hardcover edition of *The Return of the Prodigal Son* (29). Part 2 is called *Ministry and Spirituality.* It includes *Creative Ministry* (4), *The Wounded Healer* (5), and *Reaching Out* (8). Part 3 is called *Spiritual Journals.* It comprises Henri Nouwen's three journals: *Genesee Diary* (9), *Gracias* (18), and *The Road to Daybreak* (23). The goal of this edition is to issue the entire body of Henri Nouwen's work.

Anthologies/Readers

Circles of Love: Daily Readings with Henri J. M. Nouwen. Introduction and arrangement by John Garvey. London: Darton, Longman and Todd, 1988.

Seeds of Hope: A Henri Nouwen Reader. Edited by Robert Durback. New York: Bantam Books, 1989.

Show Me the Way: Readings for Each Day of Lent. New York: Crossroad, 1992. Originally published in German by Herder, Freiburg, 1990, under the title *Zeige mir den Weg: Text fur alle Tage von Aschermittwoch bis Ostern.* Edited by Franz Johna.